UNMUTED

four *[Zoom]* plays

by
Jerrod Bogard

For Miriam
Thank you for your precious time.

CONTENTS

The Birth of the Zoom Play

Togetherness was in short supply in the summer of 2020, the summer of lockdowns, of social distancing, and self-haircuts. I was bunkered in Northern Colorado, primary caregiver for my 2-year-old son, and getting all my human contact through a 16-inch LCD screen. The flurries of activity in my social media feeds made me feel simultaneously more connected and more isolated than I'd felt in my entire life. About 45 minutes before I lost my mind entirely, the artistic director of Theatre Breaking Through Barriers (TBTB), Nicholas Viselli, reached out with a writing opportunity.

Nicholas invited me to create a new play for TBTB's *Playmakers' Intensive,* a short play workshop in which I'd participated over the years when it was in-person. (Harken to the time when being "in-person" was a supposed given for plays.) This was to be the company's first *virtual* intensive. I felt confident that writing a play for Zoom was a terrible idea, but I accepted the invitation. By this point in the pandemic, I would have written a play for a cast of poodles and an audience of feral cats if it meant I got to do something creative with my friends. Fortunately for me and the poodles, there were other humans feeling the same way.

As Homo sapiens, the most social of all primates, we possess the driving need for community and connection.[1] This need has allowed us furless, soft-skinned, clawless, bipedal crybabies to conquer the natural world and proliferate as the planet's dominant species. Our

i

togetherness is not a mere preference or inclination; it is our evolutionary mandate.[2] Unfortunately, the mandates of government in 2020 seemed—at least in the short term—at odds with our instinctual nature.

Broadway had gone dark in March of that year. Under the shadow of "the Corona Virus," theatre makers around the globe were told that the show would *not* go on.[3] The closures were unprecedented in New York City, where playhouses had stayed open even throughout the Spanish flu pandemic of 1918.[4] Now, 102 years later, the lockdowns dragged on, and social distancing policies, while saving lives, threatened to drive performance venues out of business forever.[5] Meanwhile, theatre makers—all the creatives and administrators it takes to put on a play—sat at home, effectively barred from their work and their primary creative outlet.

Those of us writing plays for performance on Zoom were under no illusions about who they were for or why we were writing them. We were not trying to get the attention of agents or strengthen our resumes. Theaters would remain dark for months to come. Many venues shuttered, never to see another curtain call, but the creative spirit of artists shone bright as ever. Just as human beings have done since the discovery that animal bones cast flickering shadows on cave walls, theatre makers in 2020 used what was at hand to put on a show.

Stalwart institutions like The 24-Hour Plays, The Public Theatre, and New York Theatre Workshop reimagined their seasons for the web with programing like self-recorded monologues on YouTube, community-building town-halls on Zoom, and even performing Chekov in a video game on Twitch (respectively). Universities and actor-training programs, faced with tuition-paying students who expected performance to be part of their performance degrees, scrambled to invent a new pedagogy with acting classes and plays via computer screen. University of Windsor commissioned four new plays for the Zoom platform, and the BFA graduating class performed them in November of 2020.[6]

Prior to 2020, hardly any theatre makers had ever participated in or even heard of a Zoom play.[7] By the summer of 2020, invitations for "virtual plays" and "online readings" filled our social media feeds. By that autumn, online performances were so commonplace you could fill your week watching artists embody the phrase "the show must go on," but with one caveat—it must go on *the internet*.

Actors, famous and unknown, hosted "virtual readings" from their homes. Festivals of "online monologues" featured solo performers soliloquizing to their webcams. "Streamed plays" provided previously filmed productions from video archives. Finally, enter the "Zoom play." The newest, strangest dramaturgical invention of the era presented actors in separate speaker windows acting their quarantined faces off. Richard Nelson's *What Do We Need to Talk About*, first produced in late April, will likely go down as the first Zoom play ever.[89] The message was the medium in his hour-long play about lockdown life, a play which itself existed and proliferated by virtue of lockdown life.

Most of the writers in TBTB's virtual intensive knowingly or unknowingly followed Nelson's lead by creating plays in which the use of Zoom was part of the story. For my own part, collaborating on these plays proved inspiring and fulfilling. I felt connected with my team despite being 2,000 miles West, and the play turned out to be a piece of which I am quite proud. We shared "laughter-tears-etc.," everything you want in a good rehearsal process, but the work did more than scratch the creative itch. It inspired me and others to ask fundamental questions about our craft.

Some scholars and critics have interpreted virtual theatre, not as utilitarian evolution of form, but as a grief response, a pandemic-era ceremony of bereavement for the loss of life, livelihoods, community, and for theatre itself.[10] In a scholarly exploration of the funeral-like rites of internet theatre during lockdown, researcher and theatre professor Fenton Walsh eloquently described internet plays as "cyborg theatre," highlighting the irony that digitized theatre immortalizes performance while stripping performers of our corporeal integrity. Walsh pondered that Zoom may be "to theatre what purgatory is to heaven and hell—not the final destination, but an intermediary zone between our wildest dreams and darkest fears[?]".[11]

New York Times theatre critic Laura Collins-Hughes penned a column during the lockdown titled "Digital Theater Isn't Theater. It's a Way to Mourn Its Absence."[12] She was responding to the first wave of virtual theatre, mostly pre-recorded streams of plays filmed with multi-camera setups. Her eulogy for lost connection, while apt, ignored the thousands of playwrights and theatre-makers waiting in the wings who would, shortly after the time of her writing, parade their new works across the digital stage, not in mourning, but in celebration of life and art.

If congregation is hardwired into the human brain, then performance and storytelling are bundled and braided through those neurological structures like fiber-optic cables in the conduits of a data center. The communicative infrastructure of sound, image, language and movement run along each ceiling beam and up the support columns of our psychology. Theatre serves as the expressive documentation of our history, as an exploration of our joys, sorrows, dreams and fears, and as a practice for life's challenges. It has grown up with us from the dawn of consciousness in the forms of dance, song, puppetry, and story.[13] It has helped *create* our consciousness, our ability to comprehend ourselves and each other as existent.

Theatre (in various costumes) evolved along with human consciousness and then with civilizations, helping form our individual and collective identities, because theatre demands an audience. Just as there is no communication without a sender and receiver, there is no relationship without a perceived "other." As the pediatrician and psychoanalyst Donald Winnicott famously said (paraphrasing), "there is no such thing as a baby, only a baby and person caring for it."[14] Theatre, (the art, not the industry), is the means and manifestation of our primal, vital process of witnessing each other.

Four years after theatre venues reopened, theatre-makers continue to experiment with Zoom plays and virtual theatre. I have written four. Artists are evolving past the form's originating necessity—its genesis in isolation, uncertainty, and grief—and connecting to the joyful experience of collaborating online without the loneliness inherent in those screen-bound months when we could share time but were unable to share space. A few groups, like Virtual Arts—with founding members in three different states—are embracing the virtual theatre as their raison d'être, and I imagine more groups joining them in their commitment to further the art of virtual theatre and Zoom plays even in the absence of social distancing. While the Zoom play may never become popular entertainment, what it evolves into may one day represent the predominant form of live performance. Due to its creative potential and near-universal accessibility, its place in the independent art world is secure, and the show will go on online.

Defining the Zoom Play

"What even is a Zoom play?" asks Marian, the seasoned stage-mom in the final Zoom play of this volume. She smothers the remainder of her line in enough snark to fill a hundred conventional family dramas, *"Is it a movie? No. Is it a TV show? Sorta, but not really. Is there anybody watching? Nobody knows!"*

Defining a Zoom play as a concept distinct and separate from a conventional play, as well as from its closely related digital/internet/virtual plays, becomes important if we wish to fully comprehend the form, to discuss it with authority and specificity, and to apply criticism with integrity. Furthermore, defining the Zoom play by its own characteristics, and not merely by comparison to conventional theatre, improves our ability to study, discuss, and explore the modality. If we define it solely by comparison to in-person theatre, we judge the form through the negative lens, seeing it only for that which it is not, and risk overlooking the qualities that make it a unique performing art and a valuable contribution to culture.

Let us define a Zoom play very simply as a dramatic work conceived or adapted to be presented live via a video conferencing platform and which uses at least two speaker windows simultaneously. It is a play insofar as it shares a basic characteristic of all traditional plays: It is produced with the intent of being performed live and to be dramatized, i.e. acted out, rather than read or recited. Beyond this elemental function, the Zoom play diverges from the traditional form in the manner by which the audience witnesses the performance and by the constraints placed upon the playmakers, most obviously the geographic relationship of players with the audience and with one another. A Zoom-play's viewers watch through their personal computing devices and are (likely) not in the same physical location as any of the performers. Nor are they necessarily sharing space with other patrons. Likewise, the actors in a Zoom play do not need to share physical space during their performances. They transmit their live feed from separate spaces, often their personal, domestic spaces.

The audience/performer separation embodies the most obvious deviation from the traditional theatrical experience. Likewise, the performer/performer separation exhibits the profound difference between Zoom plays and any other mode either in-person or electronically transmitted. Indeed, the geographic separation between collaborator and witness might well discourage us from calling a Zoom play a theatrical experience at all. It is neither performed nor witnessed in a theater.

The Zoom play should be considered a subcategory of electronically transmitted dramatic works, distinct from other traditional forms viewed via the internet or television. Language scholar Timothy G. Compton, in his annual report to *The Latin American Theatre Review*, describes seeing "seven kinds of virtual theatre" in 2021, and he breaks down the shows into the following categories.[15]

Recorded Performances

- Pre-Pandemic recordings
- Mid-Pandemic recordings
- Avant-garde/experimental recordings

Live Performances

- Panels and Forums
- Plays live streamed from a theater
- Zoom-plays
- Forum Theatre

I concur with Compton's categories of internet-transmitted plays. However, as prerecorded plays are neither new nor novel occurrences, this essay will focus on live performances only. More specifically, this essay will only explore the Zoom play. The other plays, while novel for being streamed via internet, are largely unchanged but for their delivery system. The Zoom play is a new dramatic form with unique aesthetics and a burgeoning language of its own making.

Zoom plays can be divided into two categories based on the setting of the play: diegetic and non-diegetic. The term diegetic, typically used in filmmaking and film criticism, describes an element of the production (usually music) which exists in the world of the story, like a song playing on the radio that the characters are listening to, as opposed to non-diegetic, which exists outside the world of the story like the musical score the audience hears but the characters do not. In the case of Zoom plays, the diegesis (the world of the play) is either set in the video conference platform itself, (making it diegetic,) or in a fictional other-space depicted through the use of digital backgrounds (making it non-diegetic).

Non-diegetic Zoom plays can place characters anywhere—deep in a mystical forest, in a medieval castle, on the moon, anywhere—as long as the conceit is such that the characters are all sharing the same geographic location. The performers' screen windows may be arranged in a particular order by the host, giving them the ability to look "at" one another and providing the illusion of being together in space or in essence. Through creative and carefully choreographed movements, characters may appear to hand objects to one another or even embrace (although clumsily). The delivery system, being the Zoom window, or speaker window, may carry some thematic element for the piece, but may also disappear from conscious view like the television disappears from thought while watching a TV show.

Diegetic Zoom plays, on the other hand, exist inseparable from their delivery system. They place the characters and the story within the virtual conference room platform. The characters—not just the actors—are understood to be in different locations and are themselves aware they are connecting via the web.

We might also refer to these diegetic Zoom plays as *site specific* plays, where the virtual space in which they are presented is also the site in which the story takes place. The site of cyberspace, although virtual, is a site. The story takes place in the separate homes or offices (for instance) of each character but also *not* in those spaces. Inside the speaker window, inside the computer screen, scattered across an unknown number of internet servers and traveling through cable, air, and satellites, is a shared location, an agreed upon, visual concretization of the abstract, a third space occupied by matter and sound while also empty, built only of borrowed 1's and 0's and without substance enough to withstand even a tap of the index finger on a little 'x'. This third space, the virtual space, specific to each reality separately *and* collectively, simultaneously unites and divides the characters to and from one another, and the actors to and from the audience. If the viewer of the diegetic Zoom play feels alienated from the art and artists, and if the artists feel alienated from the audience and from each other, so much the better. They are conscious of the medium's message: We are apart. No dramatized story world could more viscerally depict the experience of the pandemic-era lockdown than the diegetic Zoom play.

As with all site-specific theatre, the Zoom play carries an element of immersion. Staging a production in a location diegetic to the world of the play imbues the performance with an inherent level of tactile involvement. The scenery of immersive theatre transcends the demarcation of play and audience and so becomes like surround sound for the eyes and allows one to *feel* like part of the play.[16] Viewing a diegetic Zoom play puts one in the Zoom space by virtue of the computer screen being the shared perspective of both the characters and the audience. Additionally, actors are most often presented facing full front, toward the viewer in seeming direct address, and this blocking, or staging, immerses us even deeper in the world of a teleconference (which is the world of the play.)

One further note on the immersive quality of the diegetic Zoom play: viewers bring their own feelings about video conferencing to the Zoom platform. Because the play is witnessed in the same way viewers experience a Zoom call in their real lives, (with work, family, and friends,) the play directly elicits the personal associations and history of the viewer. Conversely, a non-diegetic Zoom play asks the viewer to forget the platform and their associations with it, to make invisible the screen and fall into the story the same way we do while watching television or films.

Some Zoom play artists are experimenting with interactivity between performers and patrons. A pioneering group called Zoom Theatre (zoomtheatre.com), who produced an ambitious 11 shows between summers 2020 and '21, allowed patrons to unmute themselves in at least one production. The group primarily presented non-diegetic Zoom-plays as evidenced by their heavy use of digital backgrounds to produce the illusion of the casts' geographic cohesion. Their adventurous efforts, however, should be noted for addressing—if not overcoming—the digital chasm between the artists and the audience.

The performer/audience barrier is shared by another dramatic form derived from traditional plays: the teleplay. Teleplays, scripts for TV shows or TV movies, have historically been broadcast live in order to harness the excitement and energy of live performance for the viewers at home. General Electric transmitted the world's first live radio play, *The Queen's Messenger* by J. Hartley Manners, in 1928 to a grand total of four receivers.[17] Not long after, television viewers in of early 1950's enjoyed a vibrant array of live teleplay programming. This trend met its zenith in the critically lauded *Playhouse 90* which ran live in the '56-'57 season with scripts by pre-*Twilight Zone* Rod Serling before going live-to-tape for the next three years. In the 1990's, the Fox sitcom *Rock*, starring Charles S. Dutton, aired its entire second season live.

I remember tuning in to *Rock Live* when I was in the 8th grade. I'd never seen a sitcom performed live, and I found it electrifying. When a scene ended and they would outro to commercial break, the camera pulled back to reveal the actors breaking character and rushing off to their costume changes. Seeing them work in this way made me feel more invested in the story than ever, and more intellectually than emotionally.[*]

Unlike digital theatre, live teleplays are typically recorded in front of a live studio audience, with the live audience serving as proxy for the at-home viewer, cuing them when to laugh, gasp, or fall into rapt silence. Perhaps most importantly, the live audience provides performers a critical, real-time human reaction. Zoom play performers, in stark contrast, play to silent webcams and ring lights that give no feedback and no validation; the only human exchange of energy exists between performers.

Both the live teleplay and the Zoom play are written to be performed live for audiences who are in other locations witnessing through a screen. The most significant differences between the two are: 1) the performers in a live teleplay are sharing physical space whereas the Zoom play performers are typically separate, 2) live teleplay performers typically enjoy a live audience in the studio, 3) the live teleplay's cameras are typically operated by non-performers, whereas the Zoom play cameras are operated by the performers themselves, and 4) the entire visual aesthetic, the mise-en-scène, of the live teleplay is created by production craftspeople, while the look, location, and tone of each speaker window in a Zoom play is typically rendered by an individual performer. Both the Zoom play and teleplay are distinct from a stage play, which is conceived to be witnessed in-person and has no electronic screen between the viewer and performer. Considering all of the above, The Zoom play, although invented by artists from the live theatre, shares more DNA with the live teleplay than with stage plays.

---

[*] This is the *alienation,* or *distancing effect* Bertold Brecht cultivated through his work in the 1920's-30's.

When introducing the guidelines for Theatre Breaking Through Barriers' *Virtual Playmakers' Intensive*, Nicholas Viselli, as a seasoned actor and director, understood that writers writing for an unfamiliar medium would benefit from defined boundaries. He invoked the boundary paradox, whereby limitations increase freedom. His instruction that the plays be diegitically oriented in the Zoom space allowed writers to flex creatively within the safe boarders of an otherwise unwieldly dramatic universe. The characters in a Zoom play could be anywhere, anytime. They need not be on earth or even in this dimension, but to be considered a diegetic Zoom play, characters must be transmitting from separate geographic (or meta-geographic) spaces and utilize multiple speaker windows. What manner those windows are conceptualized by the characters or the play's internal logic makes no difference, just so long as they are recognized as part of the world of the play.

Having defined the Zoom play and some of its subsets, let's now look at how this new form has been received and perceived by the artists who have labored to bring it to maturity.

Surveys on Attitudes About Zoom Plays

In 2020, I conducted an informal survey among the online theatre community and followed up with the same questions in 2023. Along with demographic information, the survey asked how artists felt about Zoom plays across multiple domains including enjoyment, artistic fulfilment, clarity of artistic expression, accessibility, and beliefs about the artform's legitimacy and the longevity of the model.

The first survey, completed December 2020, generated 64 individual responses. The second survey, conducted two years later, generated 22 unique responses with similar demographics as the first. The surveys were conducted online, offered through social media feeds and by direct email for anonymous, self-selected participation.

Attitudes in 2020[*]

Zero of the respondents had created a play for presentation over the internet before 2020. When working on Zoom plays—compared to in-person plays—the majority of respondents reported a "little less" artistic satisfaction (75%) and a "little less" ability to collaborate effectively (60%). When asked if their work was represented as well online as in-person, there was an even split between those who felt their art was "less well-represented" and "just as well." Among the different artistic disciplines, directors felt the most positive about how their work was represented online compared to in-person, but analysis found these differences to be statistically insignificant. Regarding longevity of the form, nearly 8 in 10 respondents who took a stance agreed with the statement that "Zoom plays are here to stay regardless of pandemics," showing a resounding belief that Zoom plays are more than a stopgap measure.

Working with TBTB, a professional theatre company "dedicated to advancing artists…with disabilities and altering the misperceptions surrounding disability," creates many opportunities to discuss issues of disability. Some of my collaborators in the company have

---

[*] Percentages rounded to the nearest whole number.

expressed gratitude that Zoom "leveled the playing field," certainly by making rehearsals more accessible, but also by obscuring visible disabilities that too often become the arbiter of their character range for in-person plays. Zoom plays, they noted, expand the types of roles they are asked to play. One person shared with me that, because everyone is typically seated on zoom, the fact that they use a wheelchair had become a non-issue, whereas before it would either have to inform the character or limited their castability. Another person shared about their history with an autoimmune disease that kept them home and severely limit their acting opportunities. Zoom plays, they said, were reinvigorating their life in the theatre.

Conversations like the above inspired the idea of the survey. I hypothesized that people with disabilities might place different values on Zoom plays than the temporarily able-bodied. To my surprise, no statistically significant difference was found when comparing disabled and non-disabled artists' feelings of effective collaboration.[*] At the same time, it is important to note that the survey represents a very small sample size overall. 19% of survey respondents identified as having a disability, while the CDC estimates 27.8% of the U.S. population live with a disability.

Comparing 2020 with 2023

The most notable data of the two surveys involves the ages of the respondents. Between 2020 and 2023, the number of survey participants decreased 66%, a drip correlating strongly with respondent age. In 2020, nearly half of respondents were adults under the age of 37. Two years later, that demographic plummeted to zero.

---

[*] A chi-square test showed all p-values well above 0.05.

Not a single person under the age of 37 opted to participate in the 2023 survey. At the same time, the middle-aged group (37-60) was almost identical in participation between the two years. The other fall-off in participation was from the over-60 group. So, the missing 66% of respondents for the follow-up survey consists entirely of people under 37 and over 60.

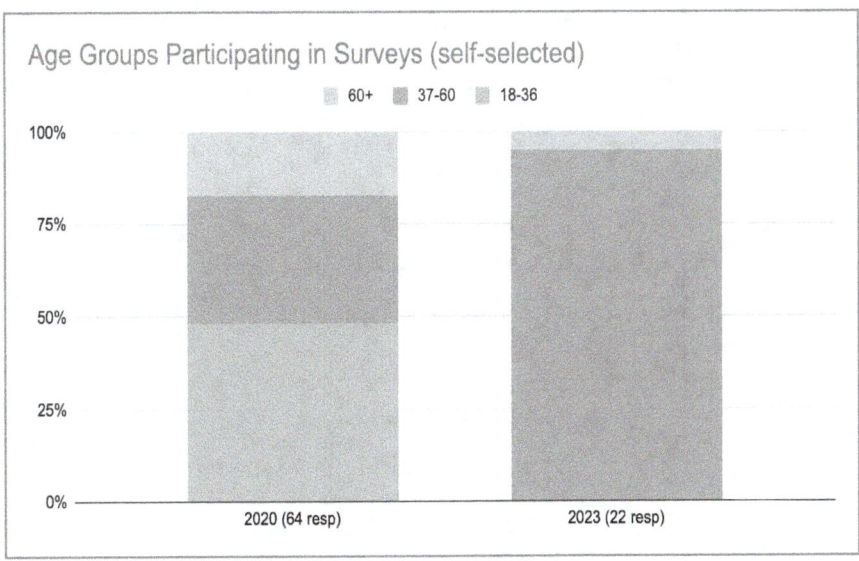

What could have driven such an exodus of the younger set? One interpretation is that the young adult group simply couldn't be bothered to fill out another survey—either because they recalled filling out the same survey in 2020, or because they had soured on pandemic-era internet surveys altogether. Another possibility is that in the two years between surveys, the young adult group took a dismissive view of Zoom plays and virtual theatre, and this attitude shift discouraged them from participating. That possibility is supported by the 2020 data showing less favorable attitudes by young adults toward Zoom plays compared to in-person plays on all three rubrics of artistic satisfaction, collaboration quality, and representation of their work. Meanwhile, older adults were more likely to report feeling Zoom plays gave them the same or better satisfaction, collaboration, and work representation.

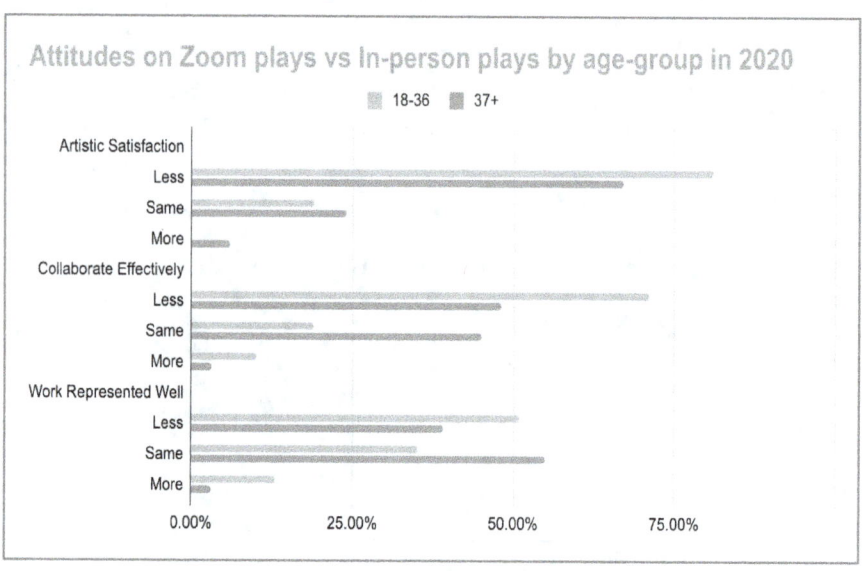

I theorize that the younger population tend to have fewer responsibilities in home and family life (i.e. caregiving duties, children, and partners,) and that this greater freedom from the tethers of domesticity allowed them to return to in-person theatre in greater numbers than the middle-aged group. Having returned to pre-pandemic patterns of life and theatre (a very busy, fast-paced lifestyle), there was simply not enough interest in the concept of Zoom theatre to invest time in a survey. While pure conjecture, I imagine that a long survey about Zoom plays was an unpleasant proposition to a young person when they could now spend their creative time engaging in the tasks and activities of in-person art.

Unsurprisingly, the two-year gap showed a steep drop off in the number of Zoom plays performed. In 2020, 98% of respondents helped create a Zoom/internet play. Only half of those surveyed had participated in any Zoom/internet plays in the 12 months prior to the 2023 survey.

The attitudes of middle-aged theatre makers became more favorable over the two years since the pandemic. Respondents age 37-60 showed an increase in artistic satisfaction. In 2023, those reporting the same or more artistic satisfaction from Zoom plays compared with in-person plays rose from 27% to 43%. As the exodus of Gen-Z and Millennial respondents indicates, the self-selected sample size of this survey has a significant impact on the data. Regarding the attitude shift on artistic satisfaction among middle-agers, it is worth considering that people who are generally more excited about Zoom plays may be more likely to fill out a survey on the topic.

Concluding Thoughts

When people collectively paused congregating in-person, the digital congregation was possible and, hence, inevitable. Many will regard the new offshoot of dramatic performance as a facsimile of "real" theatre, appreciating it for its utility but dismissing or even maligning it for its differences. But when we consider the Zoom play on its own merit, outside of the context of pandemics and lockdowns, it reveals itself as more than a stopgap or a weigh station on the return to normalcy.

Zoom plays constitute a new form of dramatic writing and a new mode of presentation on the world stage. Like the first live radio drama broadcast out of New York in 1922[18] and the first (widely viewed) live dramatic television broadcast from the British Broadcasting Company in 1930, Zoom plays and other virtual theatre will likely become a common entertainment option and, eventually, appreciated critically on their own terms and for their own unique merits and aesthetics. Unlike the radio drama and the teleplay, however, the Zoom-play is not as likely to meet the needs of audiences as much as it will the needs of artists.

Most performers (me included) have mounted plays where there were more people on the stage than in the audience, and, while we would usually prefer a packed house, the performance experience generates nearly as much artistic satisfaction in either case. Performing fulfills the drive to make collaborative art regardless of audience presence. It still "feeds the soul," and "scratches the itch." In the comment section of the 2020 and 2023 surveys, several responders wrote that the most disappointing aspect of creating Zoom plays was the lack of "connection to the audience." In contrast to these comments, artistic satisfaction was not significantly higher or lower than with in-person plays. We may surmise that virtual theatre's greatest strength is its ability to "scratch the itch" when other options are inconvenient or inaccessible. I reiterate, this "itch" is not trivial; it is an instinctive human process to be experienced and a critical need to be met.

Introductions to the Plays

In 2012, Ike Schambelan, founder and then Artistic Director of Theater Breaking Through Barriers, gathered a small group of core troupe actors and an even smaller group of contributing playwrights to their Manhattan rehearsal studio and introduced a fun idea he called *Playwrights' Bootcamp*. Pulling names from a hat, Ike grouped each playwright with a randomly selected cast. Then the playwrights would construct a new play for these actors to be read the following week. The experiment was so successful that it became an annual tradition, growing from a small table reading to a large studio full of collaborators mounting fully staged plays. After taking over as Artistic Director in 2015, Nicholas Viselli continued to expand the concept, rebranding it as the *Playmaker's Intensive* and presenting the plays as a semi-annual festival of new works.

In the summer of 2020, when the theatre world was migrating to digital spaces, TBTB reimagined the *Playmakers' Intensive* for the Zoom platform. Nicholas insisted that the plays be written specifically for Zoom and encouraged us to incorporate the interface as a part the world of the play. It is from this prompt and from the inspiration of randomly assigned players that all four of the following plays were written.

Goodnight Somebody

The first play I wrote for the video conferencing platform tells the story of a children's book author preparing for an online awards ceremony. He gathers his most trusted confidantes to preview his acceptance speech for a lifetime achievement award. His agent, his wife of many years, and the son of his beloved, deceased collaborator join the call from different cities during the height of the pandemic lockdown.

Seeking verisimilitude with lockdown life, the play meets one character while making dinner and juggling domestic and professional commitments in full view of his webcam. Steam rises from boiling pots and obscures the actor while offstage characters interrupt and demand his attention. He later moves to a private room where he whispers in order to not be overheard. Another character, when she loses her temper, is muted by the meeting host. Then she begs to be unmuted by holding hand-written notes up to the camera. These details anchor the play in that time period when we were all thrown into the Zoom world without the savvy we would acquire in coming months.

The title, *Goodnight Somebody*, references the children's book <u>Goodnight Moon</u> by Margaret Wise Brown, a favorite of mine and my two-year-old during lockdown. Among myriad mind numbing children's authors, Margaret Wise Brown stood apart as refreshing with her expansive poems and curious, often surprising illustrations. In <u>Goodnight Moon</u>, a bunny prepares for bedtime by saying "goodnight" to the day, the family, and the objects in the room. It's a melodic, dreamy meditation on object permanence. Some pages are full, edge-to-edge color illustrations, and others are tiny black-and-white drawings. On one page, you see no illustration at all—a blank page—and the text reads "Goodnight Nobody."

The main character in *Goodnight Somebody* prepares to reveal his true, queer self to his family and readers. Despite his fame and success, he describes feeling utterly unseen, invisible throughout most of his life. The play is about finding freedom through vulnerability, about the liberating, terrifying transformation from an invisible nobody to a full color somebody.

Parent-Teacher

Upon agreeing to write my second Zoom play, I was struck with the fearful thought that the form had reached its limit of creative potential. I've always disliked "talking head" drama where two characters trade quips but remain motionless, without arc, without dynamics. Zoom has the ability to put drama on ice. More honestly, I was scared I wouldn't come up with a good idea for a play. Fortunately, my previous experiences with the *Playmakers' Intensive* told me that the ideas would come as soon as I met my cast.

Estrella Tamez, an experienced actor who had worked with TBTB before, and who would eventually end up playing the mother in this piece, brought her daughter Kaisa along to participate in her first online theatre event. Kaisa was assigned to my play along with two TBTB vets, Spencer and George. I love writing younger characters, but it's a privilege I don't often afford myself because casting minors for professional plays can be such a prohibitive logistical puzzle.

Around this time at my day job, working over Zoom, I was helping teenagers and their parents navigate the struggles of lockdown life and online school. My friends who were parents were also dealing with their school-on-Zoom debacles. *Parent-Teacher* comes from these experiences. But I would not have attempted the play had Estrella not graciously joined the cast. Having mother and daughter in the same play—in the same speaker window—made the world of the play more believable and vibrant. Estrella stole the show as the prototypical Supermom: somehow both neglectful and doting at the same time.

The intergenerational sparring is my favorite part of *Parent-Teacher.* Gen-Z and Baby Boomer go toe-to-toe, no holds barred! It's a feat of dramatic dexterity anytime I can play both sides of an ideological tennis match and genuinely deliver with both voices.

Connection Restored

As is often the case, the title of *Connection Restored,* while seemingly obvious, did not emerge until after the play was fully mounted and I was able to hear the thing brought to life. The original title, *Meet Me On the Stairs*, while capturing the sentimentality of the piece, was nowhere near as pithy, apt, or familiar as the new title. It also lacked the most delicious ingredient of any title, the double meaning. I love the title so much that I debated using it for this book.

At open, we find two men at their respective computer terminals but speaking to one another on their phones and not through the Zoom portal. It soon becomes clear that they are in the same house on different floors, as one occasionally shouts off camera to be heard by the person upstairs. Their conflict? The internet is down, and the stock market is tanking. Their goal? They want to reestablish the internet and salvage their financial portfolio. When they get a three-way phone call going with a sweetly inept customer service rep., a third window appears on the zoom call so that all three men are visible.

So, is this play diegetic? Does the Zoom space represent both the stage *and* the setting? The characters' internet is down. They're speaking to one another via phone, not through their webcams. Technically, therefore, the play is non-diegetic. Nevertheless, the scene plays as diegetic. It has the atmosphere, if not the definition. The characters sit at their computer terminals as one would on a Zoom call. They know they are in separate spaces as if on a Zoom call. The frames of the speaker windows capture their separate geographic spaces. All this, combined with the characters' constant referencing of the computers, compels the viewer to feel the immersion of the setting. The play *feels* diegetic.

Connection Resorted tells a simple love story. A man attempts to save his marriage by destroying their livelihood. Here I continue a theme found in nearly all my plays. A character attempts to secure the love of another through coercion or subterfuge. The dual protagonists are gay men, but the play isn't about their queerness. It's about their relationship. The play is a lot like its author: earnest, sentimental, and a little queer. There aren't enough genuine comedies in contemporary playwrighting. I hope this counts as one.

A Moment of the Senator's Time

It's been said that the triangle is the strongest dramaturgical shape, but my favorite theatrical relationship remains the dyad. Writing a two-character play, a "two-hander," allows for a particular kind of focus and rhythm. When the writer holds only two points of view, the script's energy can build without getting diverted to a third party. Locking two well-armed opponents in verbal battle creates a potent, hypnotic energy like an exciting tennis match where you're rooting for both players. Neil Simon knew this. Edward Albee knew this.

As with the other plays in this volume, the cast was randomly selected before I put pen to paper or even thought about story ideas. After selection, the team met in a Zoom breakout room to become acquainted and get a vibe. At the first meeting, I like to ask my actors these two questions: "What types of roles do you most often get cast in," and "What role would you most like to play but haven't had the chance?" Actors sparkle in these talks. Their personalities radiate, and I bask in their energy, their style. I try to get their sent on me. Characters have a smell about them. I want to sniff out the characters hiding inside the actor.

After this informal chat, we discuss the actors' spaces. What parts of their homes or offices are they willing and able to share with the public, possibly in perpetuity? What goes on the internet must be considered eternal. Zoom plays are site specific, and the site (or the set) is only limited by where the actors are willing and able to travel with their devices. This conversation is about privacy, vulnerability, and possibility. The spaces we have available tell us more than *where* they might be; they tell us *who* they might be. Of course, the actors can always use a blank wall or a digital background, but the world of the play can be deeply enriched by the reality of the background, middle ground, and foreground. I enjoy allowing these spaces to inform my process. I feel like a chef opening a basket of mystery ingredients.

In the case of *A Moment of the Senator's Time,* the process I've just outlined had enormous impact on the evolution of this play's plot, setting, characters, and concepts. But not the twist. The twist came from my own malicious imagination, my particular brand of dramaturgical madness that—like all proper playwrights—finds joy in the futile struggle of my characters. Once again, I scream the song of love's desperate abduction.

Enjoy.

Goodnight Somebody

Production History:

Goodnight Somebody was first produced by Theatre Breaking Through Barriers as part of their virtual Playmakers' Intensive on October 30, 2020, with the following cast/crew:

Alice: Sarah Folkins
Fischer: Ward Nixon
Dianne: Jennifer Bradley
Christopher: Nick Walther

Directed by: AhDream Smith

Technical Director: Tucker Salovaara
Producers: Nicholas Viselli and Ann Marie Morelli

Setting:

A Zoom-style online meeting room with the following windows:

1) Fischer's well-appointed living room on the Upper West Side of Manhattan.

2) Christopher's kitchen and bedroom in his Brooklyn apartment.

3) Alice's cluttery, colorful home-office in Greenwich Village.

4) Dianne's rented flat in the South of France.

Characters (2w; 2m):

Fischer Williams – male, 70.
Christopher Salzman – male, 35.
Alice – female, 30-40.
Dianne Saunder-Williams – female, 65.

Synopsis:

The evening before accepting a lifetime achievement award, a legendary children's book author gathers his closest confidantes to listen to a prepared speech that may change all their lives.

Text Note:

'/' indicates for the next speaker to begin their line at this point.

(Play opens on a Zoom video conference screen with two rooms: ALICE in her home, and FISCHER in his home.)

ALICE: We can't see you. It's not great.

FISCHER: I just think that the drapes give a- a- depth.

ALICE: No, they do. But the light. It's back-lighting you.

FISCHER: But this is where the table is. You said you wanted people to see the new book set.

ALICE: It would be nice, but I mean if we can't see you, it's not a very good trade off. Do you have another light source?

FISCHER: Another—Oh, please just tell me where to be already.

ALICE: I think it has to be the couch.

(Fischer rises and begins his journey back to the couch.)

FISCHER: Where we started. I never thought I'd be providing my own set for one of these things.

ALICE: I know. It's the worst.

FISCHER: I'm a writer, not a damned...

ALICE: It's so lame.

FISCHER: ...interior decorator. *(getting seated)* Alice, do you have the uh- the order of events?

ALICE: I do. Did they not send it to you?

FISCHER: I wasn't able to print it.

ALICE: Not to worry. I have it right here. If you want, we can go over the outline real quick before your family joins the call.

FISCHER: Let's. Yes. She may divorce me when this call is over; we may as well stretch it out.

ALICE: Great. We'll get the flow of it. "The Institute of Children's Literature presents The 2020 Keats Award for Lifetime Achievement." I've got goose pimples.

FISCHER: Can we skim it, please.

ALICE: Of course. Here are the main events. Starts at eight with a welcome from the president. Then they show a video of some librarians for the Billion Books initiative. There are a few short speeches then- from authors who you've influenced- each from their homes. Boom-boom-boom and... And then it's your big introduction, which is going to be like a uh- a Ken Burns kind of slide show and it'll be narrated with the bio we worked on. Personal background, your early work with Oliver. Spends a good deal of time on the Woodland series. Roland Racoon's influence on the larger culture. They're using some of the pics you sent of you and Oliver in his studio. There's that one of you and Oliver and his son, uhm—

FISCHER: Christopher.

ALICE: Christopher.

FISCHER: Chris is the young man joining us tonight.

ALICE: I just brain-farted on his name. I'm sorry. But that picture is everything. It's the one with him on your shoulders- he must be like what—

FISCHER: He was five.

ALICE: Oh my god. And he has his little stuffed Roland, and Oliver's showing you both a painting of Roland's face?

FISCHER: It's a good photo.

ALICE: Iconic. The slide show ends on that I think. I know you're not a crier, but watch out. Hm. Also, toward the end it talks about Oliver, and it touches on his cancer. I hope that's okay.

FISCHER: You can't discuss my career without talking about Oliver. He deserves his time. *(a beat)* Are my wife and godson online yet?

ALICE: They are... they are... here. They're in the waiting room. Are you ready?

FISCHER: I think I am.

ALICE: You got this. Now it's just your wife and Oliver's son, right? We waiting for anyone else?

FISCHER: Just Dianne and Christopher tonight.

ALICE: And tomorrow the entire world.

FISCHER: And tomorrow the entire world.

(The CHIMES are heard, and DIANNE and CHRISTOPHER appear in separate windows. Dianne is in the middle of a deep drink of wine. Christopher is standing at his stove cooking dinner.)

FISCHER: Hello-hello.

CHRISTOPHER: Oh! Hey Uncle Fischer. / I'm just...

FISCHER: Whatcha doin- making dinner?

CHRISTOPHER: Yeah- you got me right as I'm- right as the baby needs to— (to offstage) What? No I got it!

ALICE: Hi, Dianne.

(Dianne raises her wine glass in greeting.)

CHRISTOPHER: *(to off camera)* To Fischer. It's started. No I am- I'm--

FISCHER: Got your hands full there.

CHRISTOPHER: No it's- it's fine. I'm- Yeah I- I guess I do a bit. But I- No I'm really excited to see you. And to get to hear the big speech! Are you nervous?

FISCHER: Christopher, meet Alice.

ALICE: Hi Christopher. We've met actually. At your dad's funeral? You were really busy, I'm sure you don't remember.

CHRISTOPHER: No-no-yeah- I- I remember now. It's good to see you.

ALICE: I think I can hear your little one in the back there. Ya know, I got to meet your dad a handful of times, all he could ever talk about was how excited he was to be a grandfather.

(A pregnant pause.

Christopher is nodding, then sees something off camera and RUNS OFF.)

DIANNE: Don't mind me. I have another bottle of wine here somewhere.

FISCHER: Hello, Didi. How is Paris tonight?

DIANNE: Paris is Paris, my dear. It's gorgeous, glib, and God, is it gay.

CHRISTOPHER: I'm back. Hey Aunt Dianne? Are you still stuck in Europe?

DIANNE: Yes, I've been *(finger quotes)* "stuck" here since February. It's an incredible hardship not being in the States during the pandemic. I just hate feeling as if the government gives a shit about me. Also the wine is terrible and the food is atrocious.

CHRISTOPHER: I can't— I know some of that was sarcastic but I'm not sure—

DIANNE: It's very late here, Darling. I'm sorry to be obtuse. Fischer, are we here to listen to a speech or what are we doing?

FISCHER: Yes. Well, this will be the speech I am going to read at the ceremony tomorrow evening. And, I am a bit nervous.

CHRISTOPHER: *(dropping a pot in the sink—steam rising)* AH! AH! Hot! Fuck. *(to off camera)* Huh!? No I'm fine! It's ready. All you have to do is let it cool.

FISCHER: Christopher, Honey, we understand if you can't do this tonight.

CHRISTOPHER: What? No! I can-- *(moving to another room)* No I'm good. I'm gonna go into the bedroom where it's— I'm working from home still. And Sarah's still got her spot at BuzzFeed, thank god, but their entire staff is from home too. Plus full time childcare so we don't even know what day it is most times. But I'm not missing this.

DIANNE: I have a question before you begin. What kind of feedback are you looking for here because you've never asked for it before.

FISCHER: All the things are virtual this year. Being so... cut off... has me feeling a little more vulnerable. I certainly never thought I'd see anything like this in my lifetime.

DIANNE: How tired are we of saying *that* this year. Take it away, My Love.

(They cheer him on- clap- thumbs up.)

FISCHER: Here goes. *(reading from paper at first)* This award has inspired a great deal of reflection for me. It professes a recognition of achievement over a lifetime. Looking over my life and at what I have achieved, it feels odd that I should be standing up here alone. Not only because my illustrator, Oliver Salzman, was more than half of every book which bares my name, but also because there is nothing good in my life that I have done alone. If we are to celebrate my contributions to children's literature, it is right that we recognize the people who made my contribution worthy: the readers, the families, publishers, and librarians who have loved Roland and let him into their homes and into their hearts. Without you I am just another ink-stained daydreamer. Without a listener, there is no story. A thing exists only when it is witnessed to exist. And I have been so fortunate. My books have gone farther and been read more than I, or any author, should ever dare dream. Yet, somehow, I feel unwittnessed. The truth is: for the vast majority of my life, I have felt invisible. To truly see someone, I believe you must see what they love. I am here now because you and I share a small thing that we each love: books and stories. I didn't create Roland and his friends. They were born from Oliver's paintbrush, from his mind and his heart; Ollie was a genius, and I stand alongside the rest of the world loving that genius. As for Oliver himself, Ollie was my collaborator, my business partner, and, for forty years, my deep and true love. If my lifetime has achieved anything at all, it is because I loved Oliver Salzman and he loved me. And any award that attempts to honor my "lifetime's achievement" is entirely void, if this fact remains invisible. I would be unseen because what I love—who I love—was unseen.

(Christopher rests his head in his hands, hiding his face from the webcam.

Stunned silence.

Is the speech over? Dare he continue?

Christopher looks up- focused off camera.)

CHRISTOPHER: *(angry, to the other room)* Please don't come in here! . . . Because Fischer is outing himself and my dad as gay lovers!

(Long pause. Everyone holds their breath.)

DIANNE: Fischer?

FISCHER: Yes.

DIANNE: *(whisper to self)* Hold it together, Didi. *(a beat - to Fischer)* Have you lost your DAMN mind!?

ALICE: Maybe we could just wait a--

DIANNE: You're asking for feedback. The feedback is, "No." 40 years you're able to keep this under lock-and-key and now you wanna sandbag us on a goddamn

Zoom call? Don't give me that look. This is not how it is done. One does not do this. To unleash something like this- like this. Alice, talk some sense into your client.

ALICE: Okay let's all just, let's all just take a breath.

DIANNE: You take a breath. I'm gonna yell.

FISCHER: Dianne. This is who I am.

DIANNE: You're damned right it is! This is very who you are. Wait until the very last possible second to drop the heaviest load of shit on everyone so they have no choice but to sit there and take it. This is CLASSIC Fischer Williams. Well, this load of shit doesn't sit. Not with me.

FISCHER: If you would like to speak rationally, I am opening to listening to your point of--

DIANNE: I should be rational? From the man about to embalm his life's work with glitter KY.

FISCHER: There's no need to be vulgar.

DIANNE: You haven't even seen vulgar. What are you going to do when they drag you through the internet? Damn it, Fischer, you know what they're going to say? Here's a preview: "Famous children's authors had gay affair." You don't like that? Here's another one for the scrapbook: "Roland Racoon is Grooming Your Children!"

FISCHER: I understand you are angry, Didi. I had hoped you would appreciate that I am finally trying to tell people who I really am.

DIANNE: Cut the shit, Fischer. I <u>know</u> you. Okay? Who you really are. The question isn't who you are, it's what are you DOING? I'll explain this subtle distinction to you because I'm not sure Millennial-Milly over here has a real grasp. Quite simply, you are making a lot of people's jobs very, very difficult. Okay? People who... hmg... people who work their asses off for you and for your "lifetime achievement." And it is not fair. It is not right. It is selfish. It is juvenile. It's a stunt. A stunt. And it's not a particularly creative one for someone who makes his living imagining ridiculous talking rodents with stupid little... *(continues talking but no sound comes out)*.

(Dianne has been MUTED, but she continues ranting while the others speak.

*Her lines below should be given space/beats as written so that the audience and characters can see and "read" her lips, but she also continues babbling unheard during other characters lines.)

ALICE: I muted her, Fischer. ... I'm sorry, I'm sorry, Dianne. I had to mute you. I think you're getting carried away and maybe that's not productive right at this moment... So let's, if we can, let's just take a minute. Let's calm down a minute. ... Fischer? Are you alright?

DIANNE: *(MUTED)* ...Am I muted? You better unmute me right now. Right f*ck*ng now! . . .

FISCHER: My goodness. Look at her go.

DIANNE: *(MUTED)* . . . M*th*rf*ck*r.

ALICE: Fischer, can I ask you--I'm sorry. Let me start here: Can I say, this is- this is- this is ballsy. I mean. Wow. And I mean you have- you have my- my- I mean you are uhm- well, you're being very brave, and--

FISCHER: Please, stop there. I don't want your congratulations. I'm not looking for sympathy. I am telling you, telling everyone that I am lucky. And if my wife will stop ranting for a minute, I'll explain that this is also an apology.

DIANNE: *(MUTED)* ... Apology? Here's what you can do with your APOLOGY.

(Dianne grabs a large notepad and a magic marker. She begins scribbling furiously.)

ALICE: So, Fischer, you've given this a lot of thought clearly. But I am wondering about what this is going to do to the launch of the box set.

FISCHER: I don't care about the box set.

ALICE: Oh. Okay, uhm. Dianne has a point though. Right? I mean a lot of people have worked really hard on this project.

FISCHER: And no one will want to buy it if I'm gay.

14

ALICE: No that's not— that's obviously not true, and also not at all what I'm saying.

DIANNE: *(Holds the sign she's made up to the camera. The sign reads:* UNMUTE ME!*)*

(A beat)

DIANNE: *(She flips the paper over, and the other side reads:* NOW!*)*

ALICE: *(a beat)* But it's not just the new printings, is it?

FISCHER: Okay, this. I expected this. Let's get it all out there. Go ahead.

ALICE: Yeah? ... The Netflix deal comes to mind. That's definitely not in stone.

FISCHER: Okay, and?

Alice: Disney on Broadway? They're still talking to us.

FISCHER: Fine, and?

ALICE: Uhm, the product tie-ins at Walmart.

FISCHER: You're grasping at straws.

ALICE: Pretty profitable straws, Fischer.

DIANNE: *(Holds up a sign that reads:* OLIVER!*)*

FISCHER: What the-- What about Oliver?

DIANNE: *(Flipping signs as Alice reads them aloud. They read:*
YOU HAVE . . . NO RIGHT . . . TO TARNISH . . . OLIVER'S . . . LEGALY.)

ALICE: *(reading the signs)* You have. ... No right. ... To tarnish. ... Oliver's ... Legally?

FISCHER: You misspelled legally. And yes, I do. You know that he left me the sole copyright.

(Dianne looks at the sign, then she scribbles on it, correcting what appears as an 'L' to what she had intended: a 'C'.)

DIANNE: *(Holds up the corrected sign, it now reads:* <u>LEGACY</u>)

(A long silence in the wake of "LEGACY". The word in big black letters remains up for a long time, hanging in the air—the writing on the wall.)

FISCHER: *(re: Legacy)* I think about it all the time.

ALICE: Fischer, we know you do. I see how hard you're working to make sure that what the two of you built lasts. I think that's what we're trying to help you do here. And, I think, that's probably why you wanted us to hear this speech tonight. Before you blow everything up. Maybe to stop you.

DIANNE: *(calmly, holds a sign that reads:* <u>Please unmute me</u>.)

(Alice unmutes her.)

DIANNE: What about the Christopher? Does he want his father's name dragged through—

CHRISTOPHER: I'm sorry. Aunt Dianne. Please, don't speak for me.

DIANNE: Then you need to say something, young man. This involves you. This is your name too.

CHRISTOPHER: I...

(Not finding the words, he resolves to say nothing for the moment, and he shakes his head.)

ALICE: Fischer. What if. How about this? What if we, as a team, as a family, we sit down and come up with the best time, the best way, for you to do this. Clearly this is very important. You want to live your truth. You deserve to. If anybody does. But … like this? Is this really the kind of ire you want to- ya know- cultivate? Is that what you're about? Is there another way maybe?

FISCHER: Is there another way?

DIANNE: He sees reason!

ALICE: So like uhm. Pride. Right? Gay Pride Day. Pride Month! New York. San Francisco. Huge. Not just a press release. We do a whole thing. We- we-we-we sponsor a float. I could sell that. Oh man, I could sell the shit outa that.

DIANNE: You could ride on the float.

ALICE: Well.

DIANNE: They'll probably make you grand marshal!

ALICE: I'm not sure if they have a... But- but- the point is we can get ahead of it. As a team we can, as a company, we can get the messaging right. Right? You have the message. But can we get the brand and the message together? I think yes. This could really make a uhm, I think, make a difference. Right? Think about it. Young people need role models. The culture needs strong examples. Representation. Packaged though. In here. By us in here. Not—

FISCHER: Out there. Not out there. I think you haven't heard what I've said. I don't feel real. In here. I want- I need- to be seen... out there.

DIANNE: I am going to say something now. And calmly. Having had five seconds to process this. Fisch, I have to tell you: I'm of three minds here. First, I am a professional woman past her prime. And they are not making it easy on us as it is. You do this, and every room I walk into there is an added layer of "oh-shit-did-you-hear?" Okay? As if thinning hair and lopsided Botox weren't bad enough. Okay? ... Second. Second, I'm your wife. I'm your wife, Fisch. You want to pretend we had some unspoken agreement where you could go off and have your lifelong love affair? That's what you need to believe, you keep that. Okay? You keep that. From this side? It sucks. That's <u>my</u> truth. ... Okay, then there's the third mind. I am your friend. Fischer, I thought I was your best friend. And even though you did not tell your best friend, I am... I am so... I'm so goddamn... proud of you. And happy for you. *(quickly dabs a tear away if needed)*. ... So what is that? That's like two "fuck you's" and a "right on, Sister?" … Alice is right.

(A beat)

FISCHER: Alright. ... Okay.

ALICE: Okay?

FISCHER: Okay. Let's... yes. We can do it your way. We will wait.

ALICE: Yeah. Yeah. Okay. Wow. Wow. What a... Fischer. That really was- is- an amazing speech.

DIANNE: I am taking my wine to bed.

ALICE: Fischer, do you want to say goodnight for now and do the speech-tweaks in the morning?

FISCHER: *(distant, sad)* Hm? What, Alice?

ALICE: You may not be feeling it tonight. You just want to... *(her phone is buzzing)* What the... And if you just want to talk, I can stay on for a little longer. What the... I'm sorry. One sec. ... What is going on? My phone is blowing up.

(Alice looks at her phone. She's transfixed. She scrolls. Her jaw drops. Her hand goes to her mouth. She opens another app. She scrolls. She GASPS.)

FISCHER: Did something happen?

DIANNE: What's happening?

FISCHER: Alice? Everything okay?

DIANNE: Where's my phone? ... What the... Holy no. Nooooooo.... WHY!???

ALICE: You already? … But… Why would you leak it? Why would do that?

FISCHER: Do what? What is it?

ALICE: It's all out there.

FISCHER: What's out there?

ALICE: This! You. The speech. It's trending on Twitter. It's on Facebook. It's...

FISCHER: What? How?

DIANE: *(aside to self)* This is blowing all my minds.

FISCHER: I haven't told anyone before tonight. Just you.

ALICE: *(reading phone)* Fischer Williams to come out as Gay at CLI's Lifetime Achievement Ceremony. Father of Roland Racoon is Gay. Famous children's author comes out of the closet at 70. What did you do?

CHRISTOPHER: I did it.

(Pause)

ALICE: What did you do?

CHRISTOPHER: I used Sarah's BuzzFeed access.

DIANNE: Ha. Hehehehe. Hahaha! HAHAHA! Oh, for the love of Milk. You are your father's son.

CHRISTOPHER: I don't think Dad would have.

DIANNE: Oh no. Not Oliver, no. I'm talking about your other father. . . . Goodnight, boys.

(Dianne LEAVES THE CALL.)

FISCHER: I want to talk to you alone.

ALICE: Yes.

FISCHER: To Christopher.

ALICE: Oh. Yes. I'll just. I'll-

FISCHER: Goodnight, Alice. Hang up please.

(Alice LEAVES THE CALL.)

FISCHER: Why did you do this? . . . Christopher. Son. Why did you do this? This is a betrayal. And I am... struggling to understand. I must believe there is a reason, that you have a reason. You're angry. You're upset, but you're, you're like family.

CHRISTOPHER: Don't say that.

FISCHER: Don't say that. Don't say... what? We're like family? But, but Christopher, m'boy, we are. We're--

CHRISTOPHER: We're not "like" family! . . . Christopher m'boy. Ya know that was—that was the all-clear when I was a kid. … I mean, after mom died. You know Dad, he, he barricaded himself in his studio. And I'd, well I would search for him in that place. Like a maze. Maze of plywood & canvases; And he was nowhere. He was the minotaur in the center of a labyrinth. And on any given school day I'd be under a table with a broken brush, I'd be scratching tic-tac-toes on the cement; and then I'd hear these hard-souled oxfords shuffle in. Christopher M'boy? Like Theseus had arrived. Uncle Fischer was here. . . . Till then it was Dad, and it was me, and we were stuck in this maze. But you came? And you slayed that monster. And dad became human. After you came, Dad became human again. The paintings stopped being walls and they became like... like windows, like bridges, ya know? Like wings. Like sky. And you did that. You did that for him. You did that for us. I thought it was a stupid—I thought it was a stupid racoon. I thought it was his work. But it was you. … So I'm not gonna let you go back. You can't go back to wherever it was you were hiding. You can't let them put you back in that maze. I won't let them do that to you. And I won't lose another Dad!

FISCHER: Honey. Breath. Take a breath, M'boy.

(Christopher takes a deep, humbling, recovering breath.)

CHRISTOPHER: I love you. And I see you. And I'm so sorry.

FISCHER: What are you sorry for?

CHRISTOPHER: I think... I think I may have ruined your life.

FISCHER: Aww. Maybe a little. But I hear that's the job of your children.

CHRISTOPHER: It's so hard right now. And I really miss him.

FISCHER: Yeah. Me too.

CHRISTOPHER: I lost him right when I wanted him most. Now you show up, I see who you are, who you've been- this whole time, and I'm supposed to let you go away again? Don't you go back down into a place where we can't see you.

FISCHER: I won't. I promise. G'night, M'boy.

CHRISTOPHER: Goodnight, Dad.

(END OF PLAY)

Jerrod Bogard

Parent–Teacher

Production History:

Parent-Teacher was first produced by Theatre Breaking Through Barriers as part of their virtual Playmakers' Intensive on June 10, 2021, with the following cast/crew:

David Dongel: Stuart Green
Kristin: Kaisa Penney
Anna Grand: Estrella Tamez
Mr. Bonchek: George Ashiotis

Directed by: Tamar Kummel

Technical Director: Tucker Salovaara
Producers: Nicholas Viselli and Ann Marie Morelli

Setting:

A Zoom-style online meeting room with the following speaker windows:

1) David Dongel's living room/office from which he teaches online middle school classes.

2) Mr. Bonchek's bedroom/office where he works when not in the administration offices.

3) Kristin's bedroom where she attends 7th grade online 4-days per week.

Characters (2w; 2m):

David Dongel – male, middle-age, middle school home-room instructor for 7th graders.
Kristin Grand – female, 12, precocious firebrand.
Anna Grand – female, middle-age, supermom with no time for momming.
Mr. Bonchek – male, baby boomer, kind-hearted assistant-principal a few years beyond retirement.

Synopsis:

A precocious tween runs the show at her latest parent-teacher conference.

Text Note:

'/' indicates for the next speaker to begin their line at this point.

(Play opens on a Zoom video conference screen with one window: DAVID DONGEL'S home office.

David is straightening up his workstation and the area in view behind him. As he walks back and forth, we see that below his shirt and tie he's only wearing basketball shorts.

He plants himself in the chair, squints at the screen to check the time and checks to see if his guests have requested to join the meeting yet. In his screen self-view, he notices his hair is askew. He tries to matt it down, but it resists. He dips his hand into his water glass and tamps down his cowlick with wet fingers.

Lastly, he grabs a bottle of Pink Pepto-Bismol and chugs a good serving. Ahhhhh. Ready.

A CHIME is heard. David hits a button and

KRISTIN and her mother ANNA appear together in a new window.)

DAVID: Hi-lo! I mean, hello. Hi Kristin. Hello Ms. Grand.

ANNA: *(to Kristin)* Okay. It's working. You got this? I'll be back in a bit. *(to David)* I have to supervise a big project I've got going.

DAVID: Oh. Okay. Are you coming right back?

ANNA: It might take a minute. Do you really need me? *(to Kristin)* Do you need me? *(to David)* She'll catch me up on what you cover. She's good about this kinda stuff. Yeah? Yeah.

DAVID: But-uhm, Ms. Grand? This is Kristin's parent-teacher conference.

ANNA: Yes.

DAVID: Right, so, you being the parent. And me being the uhm- teacher. Should we maybe, ya know, conference?

ANNA: Yes. Of course. Of course. But, Mr. uhm...

KRISTIN: *(to Mom)* Dongel.

ANNA: *(to David)* Mr.-- *(to Kristin)* Really? *(to David)* Mr. Dongel. Hm. *(aside to K)* You're right. It's weird to say out loud. *(to David)* Mr. Dongel. Hm. Can I call you David?

DAVID: *(cautiously)* SShhure.

ANNA: *(relieved)* Shew. David, Kristin and I are working on her self-management skills. Right? Self-manage. Self-starter. Because these are unprecedented times. We really need her to be able to manage her stuff and take care of things like this.

DAVID: Things like parent-teacher conferences.

ANNA: If that's what this is.

DAVID: This is that thing exactly.

ANNA: Know what? I'm here now. I may as well be here now. Right? I mean, I am the parent.

DAVID: Apparently. ... To begin with, I'll tell you that Kristin is one of the brightest students in class. I've been corralling home-room kids for, eesh, way too long, but, but Kristin is one of the smartest 12-year-olds I've ever had the... *(not the "pleasure")* ... well, that I've ever taught.

ANNA: Guess it'll be a short meeting after all. *(kissing Kristin)* Proud o' my little mini-me.

(Anna starts to go and is stopped by David.)

DAVID: But! But, as with anything good, there are a few areas for improvement. And to speak to this issue, I have invited Mr. Bonchek, the Assistant Principal, to join us this morning. And he should be here any minute now.

ANNA: Great! I have time to just run and check on my crew real quick. Call me if you need me!

(EXIT Anna.)

DAVID: Ms. Grand? Ms. Grand. Kristin, can you ask your mom to come back in? Kristin?

(With Mom out of the room, Kristin scrolls on her phone.)

DAVID: Kristin? . . . This wasn't the plan. Kristin? . . . Kristin?

KRISTIN: *(irritated)* What?!

DAVID: *(a beat)* Do we have a problem?

KRISTIN: Well, you certainly do. Turn it down a notch.

DAVID: Kristin, I'm fairly certain the Assistant Principle is going to think it's a little weird that your parent is not at the parent teacher conference.

KRISTIN: She'll be here when it matters. You're being extra right now.

(David reaches for his pink stomach medicine.)

DAVID: If you want this to go your way, I expect you to behave in the appropriate manner in front of Mr. Bonchek. Are you with me? Like we talked about?

(While David takes a long swig of the pink stuff . . .)

KRISTIN: I'll worry about my behavior. You worry about not painting the room pink with your nervous bowels.

(David chokes on the pink stuff—almost a spit-take.)

So, when does this dinosaur drag himself out of the tar pit? My people are waiting on Discord.

(A CHIME is heard: another window appears with Mr. BONCHEK).

DAVID: Mr. Bonchek. Thanks for joining us. How are you?

BONCHEK: Hello David. Hello Ms. Grand. I'm sorry for running late. Do you want to catch me up?

KRISTIN: Mr. Bonchek, I think you're still muted.

BONCHEK: Oh dear. . . Can you hear me now?

KRISTIN: You're still muted, Mr. Bonchek.

BONCHEK: Oh I thought I—

DAVID: Mr. Bonchek—

KRISTIN: It's the mute button, Mr. Bonchek.

DAVID: Mr. Bonchek you're not—

BONCHEK: I'm pushing the mute button. It's showing— Am I off or am I on? Can you hear me now?

DAVID: Yes, we can—

KRISTIN: —NOT hear you, Mr. Bonchek. Click the picture of the little microphone.

BONCHEK: Little microphone.

KRISTIN: It looks like one of your blood pressure pills sitting in a glass of wine.

BONCHEK: Yes, that's the button I'm—

KRISTIN: Does it say muted or does it say unmuted?

BONCHEK: It says unmuted.

KRISTIN: It says unmuted?

BONCHEK: Yes, it says unmuted.

KRISTIN: Okay, we can hear you.

BONCHEK: Holy smokes. Technology.

DAVID: *(awkwardly covering)* Hehehe... A blessing and a curse. Right Kristin?

KRISTIN: Oh, I'm not allowed to curse. I'm only 12.

BONCHEK: Alright. What did I miss?

DAVID: We just started.

BONCHEK: Ms. Grand, where are your mother and father?

KRISTIN: *(aghast)* What?!

BONCHEK: Am I still muted?

KRISTIN: *(tragically intense)* My dad is gone, Assistant Principal Bonchek! He's gone! Me and my Mom are on our own!

BONCHEK: Oh Dear. I'm so sorry. How long has it been just the two of you?

KRISTIN: *(matter of fact)* It's a two-day fishing trip. He gets back tomorrow.

(A beat)

DAVID: Assistant Principal, I'm sorry. Kristin's mother should be back any minute.

KRISTIN: *(calling to the next room)* MOM!!!

BONCHEK: David, I'm not sure that I'm feeling up for this today. These kids are taking it out of me.

DAVID: Here she comes. She's coming right now. Mr. Bonchek, if Kristin keeps down this path, who knows where it will lead? Right? What is it you always say? If I have. . .

BONCHEK: Helped one young person become their best self, then I am being <u>my</u> best self. You're right. This is the reason I get up in the morning. It is why I can never retire.

DAVID: *(grumble to self)* Don't I know it.

BONCHEK: *(renewed vigor)* Let's do this.

(ENTER Anna.)

KRISTIN: Assistant Principal Bonchek, this is my mom. She's really busy today because of her new startup business.

ANNA: It's a YouTube channel that streams politically themed exercise routines.

BONCHEK: *(unsure)* Ohhhh.

DAVID: Political. . .

ANNA: Exercise! Isn't it perfect? I figure we've politicized infectious diseases. We've politicized health care. The next logical step is a fitness craze!

DAVID: I guess that tracks.

ANNA: Partisan-Pilates.com! Right? And Kristin is helping me so much during this pandemic. The little darling is being her own teacher, sitter, playmate, tutor, coach, chef, mentor. She's been amazing. *(pause)* Now, I've gotta go untangle some robes from the gears of a Peloton. Assistant Principal Bonchek. Mr. uh . . . Teacher.

(EXIT Anna, awkwardly.)

BONCHEK: Did she say she was untangling robes?

KRISTIN: Supreme Court Spin Class. She's playing Ruth Bader <u>Thins</u>burg.

BONCHEK: *(a beat)* Will she, uh, be back?

DAVID: Of course she'll be back. Right Kristin? Okay. Uhm, how about we get started though.

BONCHEK: Without the parent?

DAVID: Well, just to start.

BONCHEK: I don't think it makes sense to not have the parent at a parent-teacher—

KRISTIN: What's the matter, Mr. Bonchek? Does it make you nervous to speak directly to the children in your school?

BONCHEK: Excuse me?

KRISTIN: If I make you so nervous, maybe we should call <u>your</u> mother.

BONCHEK: Alright, Young Lady, this is the kind of behavior Mr. Dongel has asked me here to address: this aggressive, antagonistic attitude.

KRISTIN: Aggressive. Antagonistic. Attitude. I can finally tell my mom I got all 'A's.

BONCHEK: Your marks will have to come up quite a bit for that to be the case. Mr. Dongel?

DAVID: *(reading from form)* 72 in English. 68 in Pre-algebra. A 63 in Art.

BONCHEK: How do you get a 63 in Art?

KRISTIN: *(shrug)* Everybody's a critic.

BONCHEK: And as for attendance.

DAVID: *(to self)* Non-existent.

BONCHEK: Ms. Grand. You have a bright future ahead of you, and I am not doing my job as Assistant Principal if I let such an intelligent, pretty girl squander her enormous potential.

KRISTIN: Did you say I'm pretty? So. . . What do my looks have to do with my potential?

BONCHEK: *(chuckle)* How much you have to learn.

KRISTIN: And I bet you're eager to teach me.

BONCHEK: I don't appreciate your tone.

KRISTIN: You're saying that my looks influence how successful I can be.

BONCHEK: I am not saying that.

KRISTIN: Oh. Then you just wanted me to know that you find me attractive.

BONCHEK: Now you're being inappropriate.

KRISTIN: Oh, I'm sorry. Am I the one who commented on <u>your</u> attractiveness?

BONCHEK: I didn't make a— Ha-ha-ha. Very good. Point taken, Ms. Grand. No, to answer your question, it does not matter at all what you look like. I was merely being nice.

KRISTIN: Nice. Well, next time just offer me some candy and a free ride in your panel van.

BONCHEK: That's— very colorful. *(to David)* You did say she has a penchant for the provocative. *(to Kristin)* Ms. Grand,--

KRISTIN: Stop calling me that. It's weird.

BONCHEK: You respect my name, and I'll respect yours, Ms. Grand. This is how professional educators operate.

KRISTIN: Okay Boomer.

BONCHEK: Okay what?

KRISTIN: Okay Boomer.

BONCHEK: Okay, let's... begin again.

KRISTIN: Okay Boomer.

BONCHEK: I don't— Why does she keep saying that?

DAVID: I believe it's a, uh., term of derision or of, uhm, dismissal.

BONCHEK: Derision for what?!

DAVID: Well for the, huh, the Baby Boomers.

BONCHEK: Ohhh, I see. Professionalism and respect are "old fashioned." Is that it?

KRISTIN: Not old fashioned. Just fake.

DAVID: Assistant Principal Bonchek, maybe this is just a generational thing.

BONCHEK: *(triggered)* I should say it is. These kids are all "too legit to quit."

DAVID: Oh no. That's not—

BONCHEK: Yes, that's right. They think being rude is "keeping it real." They think compliments are insults and insults are hate crimes. They've grown up in bubble wrap, never learning how to take their lumps, and everybody gets a trophy for simply showing up to the game!

KRISTIN: *(intensity building during the following)* Do you know why we get trophies for showing up? Because you have made it so very difficult to just-show- up. Every day, the headlines read like the prologue of a dystopian novel. The wealth gap gets wider; our margin for error gets thinner. The forests burn; the icecaps melt. Meanwhile, the police shoot at the black boys, the white boys shoot-up the schools, and the schools blame the girls' clothing for all the boys' bad behavior. It is a struggle to get out of bed, and a mystery how we drag ourselves to the game in a world that begs us, threatens us, to Just-- Stay-- Home. Your generation started us down this road, topped off the gas tank, pointed us at the fireworks factory, and put a brick on the accelerator. And now? Now you're all bailing out the side! Screaming, "They don't make'm like they used to!" *(with total disgust)* So, yes. For enduring your epic failure as stewards, as guardians, and as just plain decent people, I think the very least you can afford us is a trophy.

(Pause)

BONCHEK: I see we have a little activist here.

KRISTIN: *(emphasizing each word)* And I will not be silenced.

BONCHEK: Of course not! All you people do is make noise.

KRISTIN: Surprised you can hear it with your head in the sand.

BONCHEK: You've been to the trainings and you've memorized the talking points. But little girl, if you're an activist, I see very little action.

KRISTIN: This from a man who's dedicated his life to training children to sit down and...

BONCHEK & KRISTIN: *(together)* BE QUIET!!

(A long pause. They catch their breath.

ENTER Anna abruptly – wearing a black robe with a white doily around her neck.)

ANNA: Kris, could you— Oh you're still on. Let me know when you're done?

(EXIT Anna abruptly.)

BONCHEK: No stay-stay-stay-! . . . David. Let's reschedule.

DAVID: That probably would be best. You've had a lot of meetings. Kristin might be a little much for you to handle this morning.

BONCHEK: What? No. I can handle Ms. Grand. But-but-but it's the Mother. The parent must be present.

DAVID: Of course you're right. Also, I think the Guidance department— Mr. Rodriguez you know— being a little younger, he might find it easier making a "connection."

BONCHEK: I'll make a connection... with a plywood paddle.

DAVID: Sir, we can't do that anymore.

BONCHEK: And we wonder why the country's going to pot. The mere mention of spanking— I bet that would get the mother in here!

KRISTIN: And her lawyer.

BONCHEK: There it is! It was only a matter of time. Why do we even bother any more, David? These kids! The entitlement! The presumption! It'll be a miracle if we make it another generation. They're all so- so-. . .

DAVID: Trigger warning.

BONCHEK: . . . damned fragile!

KRISTIN: You think that because we are kind, and because we are accountable, that we are fragile? Maybe you're missing something. Maybe you didn't know that inside every kid my age, there's a tiny nuclear furnace, raging at the injustices perpetrated by the people your age. It's a miracle we haven't burned every school to the ground and that fossils like you are allowed to present yourselves as any kind of role model... for anybody!

BONCHEK: *(seething)* I have just about had it with you.

DAVID: *(softly egging him on)* Real talk.

BONCHEK: I am going to give you a little advice.

DAVID: Strait talk.

(As Bonchek begins the next speech, Kristin MUTES her computer, stands, and CALLS OFF STAGE—just like before—with her hands cupped to her mouth to project. Then SHE SITS and UNMUTES herself.)

BONCHEK: In my half a century of working with youth and with families, I have tried to instill, to impart, some sort of, any sort of discipline, respect, stability, and I have seen it all, and I have heard it all, and you know what? I am done.

KRISTIN: Just bailing out the side, huh?

(ENTER Anna, unnoticed by Bonchek.)

BONCHEK: You're damned right I'm bailing out the side! You want to make this country look like Venezuela with your feminist socialist queer agendas? Then you and all your little social-justice-warriors had better strap in, because you are going over a cliff. Over a cliff! But don't worry. I will be there at the bottom along with all the other mean old white guys who built this country . . .

KRISTIN: *'Cough'*-slavery.

BONCHEK: . . . and we will gather around, toasting marshmallows over the flaming wreckage!

ANNA: Assistant Principal Bonchek. Is it the policy of your school administration to traumatize students in their own homes?

BONCHEK: Ms. Grand, you don't even have to make the calls. Rest assured- unlike Her Majesty Kristin, The Queen of Cancel-vania, I am not too legit to quit. I am resigning as of this moment. And so, as a person who is no longer employed by the county, I can tell you both, mother and daughter, to go to hell. That will be something real over which you may howl, "Victim! Victim! Woe is Me!" Because woe is you, Ms. Grand. Woe is you indeed. Goodbye!

(He stews, breathing hard, as he searches for the "leave meeting" button on the screen. He's not finding it.)

BONCHEK: Good...bye. … Where is it?

(Still searching.)

DAVID: It's on the right.

BONCHEK: Where is it?

DAVID: It's on the lower right.

BONCHEK: I'm looking on the right!

DAVID: It says "leave meeting." It's big and red.

KRISTIN: Like your face.

BONCHEK: Jesus Christ. There! Goodbye!

(Bonchek relaxes. He puts his face in his hands.)

DAVID: Assistant Principal Bonchek. You're still here. You closed the window, but your camera and mic are still on.

> *(Bonchek SOBS into his hands for the remainder of his time.)*

Oh boy. Let me see if I can. Here, yeah. I think I can just take care of this from here. Here we go. Aaand… there.

(Bonchek's WINDOW CLOSES)

Ms. Grand? Mom-Ms. Grand, not Kristin. I'm sorry about this. The Assistant Principal is traditionally in charge of matters of attendance and discipline. Perhaps he's experiencing a little burnout.

ANNA: My God, do ya think? I mean if anyone could use some sustained cardio. But burnout or no, you just can't go talking to kids like that.

DAVID: Agree. I agree.

ANNA: What's going to happen now.

DAVID: Well, I'm actually the unofficial next-in-line for the Assistant Principal position. So, I imagine that I'll be stepping into the role. And I can assure you I am ready to meet any challenges / presenting themselves in—huh-wha?

ANNA: No. No-no-no. Not with you. What's happening with the meeting now? Are we done? Because I need this computer for an extra monitor. The guy playing Sweat Kavanaugh is obsessed with watching his own pecs bounce. *(to Kristin)* Okay? When you're done? That's my girl. *(kiss)* So pretty.

(EXIT Anna.

Pause.)

DAVID: That went well.

KRISTIN: *(a little tentative, then proud)* It worked. It did, right? Do you think it worked?

DAVID: Yeah it did. Mean, I was a little thrown when you called your mom in again. I was like "whaaa?" but you were like "we got this!" And yeah, it totally worked.

KRISTIN: So now with Bonchek out of the way, you'll be able to move up at the school?

DAVID: I think so. Yeah.

KRISTIN: *(like he's a cute kitten)* Awww. You can finally become the total tool bag you've always aspired to be. *(dryly)* My life has meaning.

DAVID: You're helping me become my best self. And that makes you <u>your</u> best self.

KRISTIN: *(laughing with him, then catching herself and returning to the aloof teen act)* Yeah-hey, before the balloons drop and the band kicks up. Remind me again how my grades are doing this term?

DAVID: Oh yes. Seems there's been an update. You have all 'A's across the board. Full Honor Role. And it's looking good for the next three terms as well. *(Thumbs up and wink.)*

KRISTIN: Perfect. And I'll see you again... When?

DAVID: Whenever. Monday?

KRISTIN: Never. I'll see you again never.

DAVID: Right. Right. Yes. 100% Attendance Award "unlocked!" Cool. Cool-cool-cool.

KRISTIN: Right. Well. I guess… bye then.

DAVID: Hey, Kristin? You know when you were laying into Bonchek back there? Really going for his throat?

KRISTIN: Yeah?

DAVID: For a second there, I saw your eyes… light up. It's moments like that when I really know why I became an educator. Thank you.

(END OF PLAY)

Jerrod Bogard

Connection Restored

Production History:

Connection Restored was first produced under the title *Meeting On The Stairs* by Theatre Breaking Through Barriers as part of their Virtual Playmakers' Intensive on November 14, 2022, with the following cast/crew:

Anozie: Khalil LeSaldo
Danny: Stephen Drabicki
Ben: Jack Sims

Directed by: Richard M. Rose

Technical Director: Tucker Salovaara
Producers: Nicholas Viselli and Ann Marie Morelli

Setting:

3 settings seen through a Zoom-style online meeting room with the following speaker windows:

1) Anozie's home office.

2) Danny's home office.

3) Ben's home office.

* Note on Setting: Although the characters are seen through their computer cameras, the characters are *not* in a Zoom call. They are connected via phone only.

Characters (3m):

Anozie Azubuike – male, 30's, day trader working from home. Keen, assertive, controlled— until he's not. American-born of Nigerian descent.

Danny Barnnett – male, 30's, Anozie's husband. Also a day trader working from home. Entitled and critical— until he's not.

Ben – male, 50's, a technician at the internet provider's customer service call center. An old hippie, intelligent, calm, kind, a bit out-to-lunch.

Synopsis:

A married pair of day traders seeks help with their internet connection during an international financial crisis.

Text Note:

'/' indicates for the next speaker to begin their line at this point.

(Play opens on a Zoom video conference screen with two speaker windows: ANOZIE and DANNY in different rooms/screens.

*They are not speaking into the screens. They are not "on" a zoom call. They are on the phone with one another. The zoom windows are simply the point of view of the characters' computers and our window into their world.)

ANOZIE: Hey you there?

DANNY: I'm here. I've been here.

ANOZIE: Why didn't you say anything?

DANNY: I did say something!

ANOZIE: Okay let's not-let's-not-let's-not. Just- *(a breath)* Just gimme a sec and I'll get the guy on my end and then I'll join the call. Okay?

DANNY: Okay. Yes. Yes. Okay. I'm waiting. As usual.

(Anozie uses his phone to set up a three-way call.)

DANNY: The market is gonna balance. Can we take a breath? . . . Why don't we do this in the same room? *(yelling to the lower floor in the house)* Why are we not in the same room!? This is stupid!

(Danny puts down his phone and EXITS his room while continuing to complain audibly. He walks out of the frame of the video window. Danny's video window now shows his empty office.)

ANOZIE: Just wait! When it's ringing I'll hit the— *(to Danny off camera in his room)* Why are you down here? You have to be at your desk!

DANNY: *(off stage unseen)* We don't have to be apart right now!

ANOZIE: We do unless we want to be running up-and-down the stairs like idiots. If we're in both rooms, we can troubleshoot and it'll get fixed faster. What if it comes back on upstairs but it's still offline down here? Then we gotta get back on the phone and do this all over again? Daniel. *(noticing his phone)* Just lost another 100 points. Danny- please.

(Anozie finishes typing in the phone number to his phone and then joins the calls.)

Okay it's ringing. ... I joined the calls. Are you there? ... Danny? *(yelling upstairs)* Daniel!?

DANNY: *(ENTERING his screen, grabbing his phone)* Here, I'm here.

ANOZIE: You hear it ringing?

DANNY: I hear an enormous toilet flush, and tens of thousands of dollars getting sucked into the sewer.

(BEN appears in a new video window. He uses a headset/mic, wears a tie-dye t-shirt, and there's a cereal bowl next to him.)

BEN: Thank you for reaching out to Net-Opti-Tela Solutions. We value you and your business because / we know—

DANNY: Whooooshhh

BEN: *(a beat)* Hello?

ANOZIE: Hello-yes. Our internet's not working and we really-*really* need to get it back as soon as absolutely possible. Can you help make that happen, Sir?

BEN: Absolutely, man. Yeah. But uhm, would you mind if I uh- if I get through this greeting?

ANOZIE: What? No-no-no. We can skip all that if that's alright. We're in a rush and we just need back online so we can get back to work. So whatever can you do like, on your end, and get it going, please do.

BEN: Yeah. Yeah-yeah-yeah. It's just that it's- well it's tied to my bonus eligibility. To uh, ya know, do the whole thing.

ANOZIE: What?

BEN: The greeting thing?

ANOZIE: Okay fine yeah. Just get us through it.

DANNY: Flush.

BEN: D'you remember where I left off?

ANOZIE: Just do the whole thing. It's fine. Just quick.

BEN: Well. You're in a hurry. I don't wanna make you wait.

DANNY: Considerate.

BEN: Thank you . . .

ANOZIE: Great so we / can-- hm?

BEN: *(reading)* . . . for reaching out to Net-Opti-Tela Solutions. We value you and your business because we know you have a choice when it comes to the network you choose. My name is Ben. May I have the first and last name of the account holder, please?

ANOZIE: Anozie Azubuike.

> *(A long beat as Ben types a few letters into his keyboard and then stalls out...)*

Hello?

BEN: No that's fine. Uhm. Would you mind uhm

ANOZIE: Starts with 'A' as in Alpha. November. Oscar. Zulu. India. Echo. Ready for my last name?

BEN: Oh you're spelling it. Thank you.

ANOZIE: Ready for the next one?

BEN: Oh no- I need that first one again please.

DANNY: You had to put it in your name.

ANOZIE: Don't start, Danny. Danny don't start.

BEN: Oh, Danny? That's much easier. Danny, what's your last name.

DANNY: It doesn't matter, does it?

BEN: But I need it to get into the account.

DANNY: It's not in my name. It's in my partner's name.

BEN: Okay.

DANNY: Anozie Azubuike.

BEN: Okay. That's the name?

ANOZIE: That's the name the account is under. Yes.

BEN: Can you spell that?

ANOZIE: I *can* actually.

BEN: Oh thank God.

DANNY: It's spelled A as in apple.

BEN: *(typing)* Okay.

DANNY: 'N' as in Nancy.

BEN: K.

DANNY: 'O' as in Online.

BEN: Got it.

DANNY: 'Z' as in Zero.

BEN: Got it.

DANNY: 'I' like Inevitable.

BEN: Good word got it.

DANNY: 'E' as in Ending. Anoz, will you do the rest?

ANOZIE: Azubuike. Spelled—

BEN: Wait- I'm sorry was that your first name or your last?

ANOZIE: *(calm through gritted teeth)* Azubuike is my last name. *(a beat)* Hello?

BEN: Would you rather I look up the account using your phone number?

ANOZIE: Are you fucking—*(breath)*.

DANNY: Can you see the phone number we're calling on?

BEN: I can.

ANOZIE: That's the phone number.

BEN: That makes sense. *(typing)* Got it. Can you verify your billing address please?

DANNY: *(fast)* 1428-Ceder-Street-Northwhich-New-York-12812.

BEN: Alright. ... What can I help you with today?

ANOZIE: Just gotta get back online, Ben. We gotta get back online.

BEN: Alright. Well, I'm sure we can get you back up in no time. What seems to be the issue?

ANOZIE: There's no internet, and we're going broke. Every second we're going more broke. Please tell us how to get the internet back on.

BEN: You guys work from home?

DANNY: When the internet is working. Which it always did before we became hillbillies.

ANOZIE: Daniel.

DANNY: Never went out in Chelsea. All I'm saying.

ANOZIE: Have you said it enough?

DANNY: Have you heard it yet?

BEN: Okay well the first thing. Hm. *(munches a spoonful from a cereal bowl)* Yeah the first thing is trying to do a hard restart. Have you tried unplugging it, waiting 30 seconds and plugging it back in?

ANOZIE: We tried that three times. Yes. Both routers.

BEN: And what happened?

ANOZIE: Same problem.

DANNY: Nothing changes, no matter what we do.

BEN: Alright. Let's run through the usual suspects.

ANOZIE: Run run run.

BEN: Okay. I'll run a diagnostic on this side. And while that's working, tell me when your connection went down, and if any other power outages occurred at the same time. Charlette! Get down! Down! Sorry, fellas. My roommate. ... My cat is my roommate.

ANOZIE: Ben, right?

BEN: Yup. Ben.

ANOZIE: Okay Ben. We are literally losing money every second this problem persists. Okay? We're traders. Stock traders. We have active trades. And I don't know if you're watching the market. But it's a terrible day to be a trader with no internet. Okay? So let's please stay focused.

BEN: Yeah yeah. Of course. I haven't been watching the market, though. Is it doing something?

ANOZIE: Please. Ben. Internet.

DANNY: Don't fight him, Ben. He always gets his way.

BEN: No of course not. Let's get this done. So okay. That diagnostic is finishing up. Did anything happen at your place right before you lost connection? Oh, and are you in an apartment or a house?

ANOZIE: A house.

DANNY: A great big, beautiful, old Victorian. A real dream home right out of Martha Stuart Magazine.

BEN: That's... great. Do you know if you share the same service line as your neighbor or if it's a dedicated line?

ANOZIE: Dedicated.

DANNY: Hardly any neighbors at all 'less we count the shut-ins and the summer-homes down the hill.

ANOZIE: That's not helpful, Danny.

BEN: That's actually pretty helpful, Danny. Rural areas like where y'all are at- it's a real netty-spagetti kinda situation. There can be split-offs, cut-offs, daisy-chains connecting houses, some people are able to run a dedicated wire all the way from a major population center. It's a real... Charlette! Ahh I hate to scare him. He's not seeing very well and gets jumpy. Okay there we go. The diagnostic's in here. And okay... it's showing that it's running on our side. The area. All the way to the junction box at the corner of county road 302. Did y'all have a storm? No? So most likely it's the modem isn't responding.

DANNY: So it's like the internet keeps talking and sending signals, but the modem isn't listening? Just can't hear it, no matter how clearly the signal is sent?

BEN: Have you tried unplugging it and plugging it back in?

ANOZIE: Yes! Yes! We tried unplugging it and plugging it back in! Upstairs and down!

BEN: Oh you're running on two routers? Same network?

ANOZIE: That's right, yes.

BEN: You unplugged both of them?

ANOZIE: Yes.

BEN: And did you plug it back in?

ANOZIE: Yes!

BEN: Both of them?

ANOZIE: Yes!!

BEN: And did that work?

ANOZIE: *(a beat)* NOO!! . . . Is there a- a- a- work-around? Something we can do just to get on in the short term? It's like black Tuesday out here, Ben. We have got to get online. I can't even call my broker because all the goddamn account information is- guess where- online.

BEN: Well, man. I mean there's- I guess there's always your cell phone. Have you tried tethering your phone as a hotspot?

ANOZIE: Yes, we tried that.

BEN: Did that work?

ANOZIE: No it didn't work! If it had worked, I'd be saving my retirement fund, not listening to you scream at your poor blind cat!

DANNY: It's the cell reception, Ben. We get like one bar out here. It's like, enough to talk, but it won't run the computers. It's a pretty desolate environment, culturally speaking.

ANOZIE: Enough, Danny. I see you.

BEN: Am I really screaming? Oh God. Oh man, I'm sorry Charlette. Come here, pus. Ps-ps-pss. Here buddy. Daddy's not trying to be mean. No.

ANOZIE: So the internet.

BEN: I have to give this furry guy eye drops like four times a day, man. You ever try to give a cat eye drops? It's like... stressful, man. First you gotta wrap him up in a towel to keep him from clawing your face off. Then, if you can get that done, and after he's all rolled up like a cat burrito, ya still gotta keep his little head from turtling back into the towel. And yer holdin him under your arm, kinda squeezing him like yer playin the bagpipes, and he's, well he's just weezin and yowlin, so it sounds like St Patrick's day in hell. And then, well, then you gotta get him to open is eyes! And with this dropper comin in at him! Yer pullin his fuzzy forehead back. His gums are all rrrrr... so it looks like his face is gonna peel off. Eyes are all ghost white & glassy. And you're thinking- this can't be how the pros do it. It just can't. And that's when you hear it- the demon breath. He starts this- this like- weezy thing- but real heavy and just through his nose, ya know? *(mimics the cat breathing heavily through his nose.)* And it has got to be done. And you know it has to be done. Charlette, it's got to be done, sweety. Because Daddy loves you. *(sigh)* It's hard being a parent. D'yall have kids? *(bite of cereal).* Or oh—when you said partners did y'all mean just business partners. Anymore I guess I really don't know what people mean when that say partners.

(A beat)

DANNY: Neither do I.

ANOZIE: What just happened?

DANNY: We don't have kids.

ANOZIE: Yet. But we're-we're working on it.

DANNY: Sure. I mean supposedly it's why we moved out to the sticks, Ben. Abandoned our friends, our community, my work. I mean not <u>only</u> to spend my inheritance on a new roof and basement repairs. But also—ya know—supposedly— to uhm, have a family.

ANOZIE: You have to give something up to get something great.

DANNY: Oh trust me, I know.

ANOZIE: What the hell are we talking about? We are going to be ass out with no roof, no basement, and noting in between. Okay? Guys? So, eyes on the prize?

DANNY: What is the prize, Zie?

ANOZIE: What's the—what are you talking about 'what's the prize?'

DANNY: So we get online. For what? Then what?

ANOZIE: What? I can't with you right now. Talk to me, Ben. What are you gonna do about this? Because I'm about to drive to town and find a damn Wi-Fi connection. And if I have to sit in a damn cracker barrel parking lot, I will do that.

BEN: Ya know, man, I mean if it's that important, it actually might not be a bad plan.

ANOZIE: Okay, that's fine. And after I save us from complete financial ruin– ehem– "the prize"– I'll probably call your supervisor and do my absolute best to have you fired. How's that sound?

BEN: It doesn't sound good.

DANNY: That's not your prize, Zie. Saving the day like you're the superhero wolf-of-Wall-Street. Come off it. Your prize is this: it's you and me sitting up here in the woods like a couple of rainbow Adirondack chairs, you in your room and me in mine, making pretend money and more pretend money and more pretend money so we can pour it into this fantasy doll house to impress I-don't-know-who. Your family? Our friends—like we have any of those left—till we get old, die, mummify, and fossilize after I slit my wrists in that goddamned antique claw bathtub!

BEN: *(a beat)* That sounds like a terrible prize.

ANOZIE: Okay. Babe? I think you're clearly under a lot of pressure. And there's some stuff we need to talk about. Okay. But is this the moment?

DANNY: It's never the moment! It's never the moment.

ANOZIE: Danny! We get it! And as usual you're making it very clear to anyone who will listen that you're very unhappy. And, as usual, I'm just trying to hold this whole thing together as it's flying into pieces. So please! Ben is the I.T. guy. He is not our therapist. Let's let him do his job, which is to make- the internet-work!. Right?! Ben?!

BEN: Yeah, man. I'm trying to help you guys. But, did I hear right? Danny, you work in the upstairs office, and An-o-zie—

ANOZIE: Just say 'Z'.

BEN: Z, your office is separate —

ANOZIE: I'm downstairs, yes.

DANNY: And ne'er the twain shall meet.

BEN: Okay. I think I'm getting the picture. I mean I think I see what's might be <u>really</u> happening. Can I ask you both a serious question?

DANNY: Yeah?

ANOZIE: Okay.

BEN: Is the green light on your routers blinking?

ANOZIE: Uhm, Danny. Are you looking at your router?

DANNY: No, I mean yes I am, but it's not blinking.

ANOZIE: Mine's not blinking either.

BEN: Okay. So, tell me, each of you. What are they doing?

ANOZIE: Mine's just on solid. It hasn't changed.

DANNY: Mine is also on solid, but there's two other orange lights on solid as well.

ANOZIE: Just fix it, Ben! What the hell am we paying 80 bucks a month for and we can't get online to do our damn work?

BEN: 80 bucks? Holy crap. Let me get y'all on a better plan.

ANOZIE: The DOW just dropped another 200 points! Make the internet work!

BEN: Right-right-right. Okay. Based on what you're telling me, I think I know the issue.

DANNY: You do?

ANOZIE: Yes!

BEN: Yeah so, your routers. I'm pretty sure they're busted.

ANOZIE: What do you mean "busted?"

BEN: *(definitively)* I'm mean like busted.

ANOZIE: Oh you're serious. Well- Okay- so- so- so what do we do? I mean I guess I should just go then, right? We should just take our computers and- before we lose any more time, right? Danny?

DANNY: I broke the routers.

ANOZIE: What?

BEN: Oh, Danny!

ANOZIE: What? What do you mean you— what are you— wait—What?

DANNY: I did. I busted the routers.

BEN: *(vindicated)* So they <u>are</u> busted.

ANOZIE: What did you do?

DANNY: I poured kombucha on them. I drown them in kombucha.

ANOZIE: *(unbelieving, a beat)* My kombucha? That you said you drank by mistake?

DANNY: Your kombucha that I said I drank by mistake.

ANOZIE: *(totally thrown for a loop)* Wha- wh- why?

DANNY: Because I hate kombucha.

ANOZIE: So you... ruined our lives?

DANNY: No. I ruined our lives because I hate our lives.

ANOZIE: I know that! You complain about every goddam thing all the time! But why didn't you just leave! Why this? Why... TODAY!?

DANNY: Because I love YOU! I hate this life and I hate what you've become with this office and this house and this soulless, meaningless, day-trader bullshit that I even followed you on. So stupid! But I followed you because... I love you! But I shouldn't have! I should have pushed back. I hate what it's become. What you've become. What I'm *becoming*. But I love YOU! And I love US! But the us that we *used* to be. Before all this, this, this stupid story we've been telling here, whatever this-this-this... *THIS* is. I just want you. I want you, and a tiny apartment, and our friends, and yes. Let's have a baby, but we can do that anywhere. We don't need the queer Norman Rockwell family portrait! And yeah. Yeah! I could have left. Yes, I could have left, but I couldn't get you to look up from the charts and a hundred monitors long enough to know I was gone. It has this... hold on you. Some kind of strangle hold and I feel like I'm fighting it. I'm fighting the house, I'm fighting the décor, I'm fighting the work, I'm fighting the fucking market! I'm fighting it all,... just to get you, YOU, ANOZIE AZUBUIKE, back. So yes. Fuck your routers. That's how much I love you. Fuck. It. All, Zie. And Kombucha is gross so stop it with that shit.

(A long beat. Anozie breathes. He's been dragged. He's putting it all together.)

BEN: Azubuike. Once you hear it enough times, it's not that complicated to spell.

ANOZIE: *(absently)* Bye Ben.

BEN: *(racing to read his script)* Oh, we thank for choosing Net-Opti-Tela. We know you have a choice when it comes to da-da-da yeah. So you're going to get an email survey asking about your service today and it would be—

(Anozie pushes a button on the phone and Ben's screen disappears—EXIT Ben.

Anozie and Danny remain on the phone together — still in separate rooms.)

ANOZIE: Daniel?

DANNY: What? Tell me the NASDAQ tumbled another thousand?

ANOZIE: Why are we not in the same room?

DANNY: I agree.

ANOZIE: I'll meet you on the stairs.

(They each drop their phones and rush out of their rooms. The rooms sit empty for a few beats.

END OF PLAY)

A Moment of the Senator's Time

Production History:

A Moment of the Senator's Time was first produced by Theatre Breaking Through Barriers as part of their Virtual Playmakers' Intensive on April 28, 2025, with the following cast/crew:

Cheryl/Marian: Mary Ann Conk
Dena/Rose: Rachel Handler

Directed by: Ashley Wren Collins

Technical Director: Tucker Salovaara
Producers: Nicholas Viselli and Ann Marie Morelli

Setting:

A Zoom-style online meeting room with the following speaker windows:

1) Dena's home office.

2) Cheryl's home office.

Characters (2w):

Cheryl (and Marian) –female, 68, professional, dignified, tough as nails.

Dena (and Rose) – female, 38, professional, vulnerable, but determined.

Synopsis:

A middle-aged woman finds she must go to battle with a trusted mentor for her dignity and respect.

Text Note:

'/' indicates for the next speaker to begin their line at this point.

(Play opens on a Zoom video conference screen with two speaker windows: CHERYL's clean and well-appointed living room, and DENA's home office.)

DENA: Hello, Senator.

CHERYL: Oh, we're being formal.

DENA: How are you?

CHERYL: And we're doing pleasantries.

DENA: I didn't quite know how to start.

CHERYL: Look, we both have busy lives. I'm playing catch-up to Cunning's half-dozen super PACs, and the weasel's lead gets bigger every second I spend on Zoom calls with former staffers who are suing me. And you, well, I'm sure you have some camp-fire sing-a-long to get back to. Not sure what they get up to at those socialist shindigs, but it must be worth it for you to have jumped ship on a 10-time incumbent with one ass cheek in the speaker's chair. That enough chit-chat for you?

DENA: Absolutely.

CHERYL: Sooner we do this, sooner I get back to the work of the people, and you get back to plotting your next mutiny.

DENA: That's... unfair.

CHERYL: Unfair.

DENA: It's an unfair characterization of how things transpired. Yes.

CHERYL: Fairness. Alright. Let's circle back to fairness in a moment. Why don't you tell me what this call is even about so that I can tell my attorneys why they are not on it. And by the way, I do not give permission for you to record this call, and yes, I AM recording *(holds up an iPhone)* because, well, once bitten. So what's up, Dena. Lay it out there.

DENA: Can I talk now?

CHERYL: Finally. Please.

DENA: Are you sure?

CHERYL: I'm sorry. Am I being abusive?

DENA: My attorney says abusive is the technical language for what happened.

CHERYL: Well, tell it to Fox News, Dena. And tell me why we're here. Every second I put into this is good money after bad.

DENA: I think a few minutes of your time is the least you owe me after the work I've done for you. The multiple times I've saved your butt.

(Long beat — No response from Cheryl.)

I didn't mean for it to leak.

75

CHERYL: Mean for it to leak. It didn't have to leak. Filing a lawsuit is public record, my dear. Or was that not part of the Political Science curriculum in your fancy graduate program?

DENA: I was angry. And I had a right to be.

CHERYL: That is the line. She's an angry young woman with... *(reading from paper)* "a chip on her shoulder and something to prove, but it is unfortunately misplaced anger stemming from long-ignored mental health issues. We unequivocally disavow the hurtful and untrue accusations made by this confused and unwell person." We got that one out in record time, and somehow in the absence of my head legislative staffer.

DENA: That was,… not right.

CHERYL: No? It's not right? Having a trusted colleague run your name through the mud?

DENA: No, it's not right to have run-on sentences in your press release. Sounds like ChatGPT was snorting Adderall.

CHERYL: Drug use. Maybe that goes in the next talking point.

DENA: Senator. Cheryl. Are you at all curious as to why, why I left the way I did? You don't see anything wrong with the way I was treated? The way that you —

CHERYL: Stop-stop. Stop right there. This is why, when they heard I was taking this call, my lawyers had syncopated angina attacks. Sounded like dogs barking Jingle Bells. . . . What. Do you. Want, Dena?

DENA: I want to settle.

CHERYL: Okay. People in hell want an elevator pass. So?

DENA: I will settle.

CHERYL: Okay. For?

DENA: For an apology. Right here. Right now. Just you and me. An apology.

(Cheryl changes tone here. Cheryl drops character, breaks the scene. She is now MARIAN.)

MARIAN: An apology.

(Dena pauses. Confused for a second. Shakes it off.)

DENA: For an apology. Right here. Right now—

MARIAN: *(More intensely articulating.)* An apology.

(Dena changes tone here. She drops character as well. She is now ROSE.)

ROSE: We're in the middle of our scene? Are you correcting my pronunciation?

MARIAN: You're ENUNciation. You sound like you're saying foreign pology, or foreign policy.

ROSE: *(irritated)* Okay. Fine. An_ apology. Can we keep going? We're right up on the end.

MARIAN: Well I can't tell.

ROSE: Can't tell what?

MARIAN: You can't tell the end is coming because it's not building. It's not building because you're not matching me for the intensity and pace, and you're swallowing your lines.

ROSE: Jesus Christ, Mom. Did I personally offend you by asking you to be in this play?

MARIAN: Oh a play. Is that what this is?

ROSE: Wow. What is wrong with you? We were fine. You were fine like ten minutes ago.

MARIAN: I'm sorry. I'm sorry. It makes me *livid* when a good actress picks up bad habits. I've been holding it in all day, but. There. I said it. It's past. Let's continue.

ROSE: Oh, we can continue now?

MARIAN: I said let's continue.

ROSE: *(a beat)* What bad habits?

MARIAN: It's past. Let's move on.

ROSE: What bad--

MARIAN: It's past. I said sorry. Let's move on.

ROSE: If you tell me, I can fix it.

MARIAN: No, you can't. It's too late.

ROSE: It's rehearsal.

MARIAN: Honey. Rose. You don't fix years of instrument degradation in an afternoon, on Skype.

ROSE: It's Zoom.

MARIAN: Sweetheart, to an old hoofer like me, all this nonsense is Skype. *(to herself)* "Virtual" play. How did I let myself get talked into this?

ROSE: Well, I'm sorry, Mom. I'm sorry I'm not the Great Sarah and I'm sorry on behalf of the internet and the 21st century. I'm sorry that art forms shift. And I'm sorry that I wanted to do something fun and creative with my mother.

MARIAN: You don't have to be dramatic.

ROSE: I'M being.

MARIAN: I never said you have to be Sarah Bernhardt. For God's sake. As if you could. *(a beat, then realizes she crossed a line)* As if *anybody* could. I was doing you a professional courtesy. Treating you as a professional. Isn't that what you want?

ROSE: Oh that was professionalism. Okay, I wondered what that was.

MARIAN: Everybody needs to hear the truth, and if your fellow actors can't tell you, then whose job is it?

ROSE: Your Mother's, evidently.

MARIAN: I was simply pointing out that your craft has slipped, and it is a tragedy—

ROSE: A tragedy. And I'm being dramatic.

MARIAN: Because once-upon-a-time in New Jersey there was a little girl who showed / so much promise—

ROSE: Please don't.

MARIAN:: —so much promise, that casting directors

MARIAN & ROSE: …were hiding in the bushes.

(Marian raises her eyebrows and gives a look and hand gestures that say, "well, I speak the truth.")

ROSE: Okay. Well. R.I.P., little pig-tailed New Brunswick girl. I will strive to make you proud with my elocution, my posture, my pace and my personal hygiene. Will that make you happy? And would that make you read the dang play?

MARIAN: If you would care enough to actually do all that, then I'd be connecting you to Gene and you wouldn't need to be cat-fishing plays on the internet.

ROSE: I'm what? What are you even saying?

MARIAN: I will make you a deal.

ROSE: The deal again?

MARIAN: If you start taking your craft seriously, then I will vouch for you and get you into the rooms. First thing is start using your real name again. My God. Like being stuck in hell and throwing away an elevator pass.

ROSE: *(to herself)* That's where I got that.

MARIAN: How do you think this makes me feel? I worked for five decades building the respect on our family name. It's not a famous name, but it doesn't have to be famous to be known. Known is better than famous in fact, because it can't be fucked up by the well-meaning public and the wanna-be's.

ROSE: You said it would make you proud if I could build a name on my own.

MARIAN: Well, you are getting to a certain age now, dear, and that path is clearly not for everyone. So, the deal is, change the name, start taking your craft seriously again.

ROSE: I take my craft seriously.

MARIAN: Your resume doth protest. And I'd call Gene or I'd call Terrance at the Playhouse today if I didn't think you'd march in there and start swallowing your 'T's.

ROSE: I don swallow my 'T's.

MARIAN: Oh, don' you?

ROSE: I don'T. AAGHG!!

MARIAN: Support dear. You'll get polyps. ... You think it's all fun and I'm being a silly old bitch, but this is what a career on the stage can get you if you work hard, take it seriously, and take yourself seriously.

ROSE: What does it get you? A raging case of Narcissism?

MARIAN: You know who's a narcissist?

ROSE: Who?

MARIAN: Anyone who's got more than you. Don't take that road, Rose. You're better than that. What it gets you is a condo with a view and something to rely on when it's time to rely, because you can't count on the world. Tell me I'm wrong.

ROSE: You're not wrong. Listen. I hear you.

MARIAN: I'm saying all this because I care, sweetheart. I'm your mother.

ROSE: So you've said.

MARIAN: Excuse me? What did you say to me?

ROSE: No. I know. I know you love me. I know you're just—

MARIAN: I'm "just". My God. I lost an entire summer stock season and had to start playing big-hipped nurses because I "just" gave birth to you. And I'm "just" willing to put my name and my reputation on the line, again. And I just skipped a lot in between there.

ROSE: Oh, I know you did.

MARIAN: Would you like me to go back?

ROSE: Please don't.

MARIAN: Because I could.

ROSE: Aren't you even a little curious?

MARIAN: About what?

ROSE: About my play. Where it goes? How it ends?

MARIAN: We were talking about your career. Why are you talking about the play?

ROSE: Because I wrote a fucking play, Mom! I wrote a play. I wrote a play. Did you ever write a play?

MARIAN: Oh God no. *(a beat)* And have a bunch of amateurs mumbling through my lines while I cringe in the back? No-no-no. But if I did, I tell you what, I wouldn't let them do it on Skype.

ROSE: On Zoom.

MARIAN: Yes, of course dear. On Zoom.

ROSE: It's a play. I wrote it.

MARIAN: I know honey. And it's really not bad. It's just—

ROSE: Finally. What?

MARIAN: Well.

ROSE: What!?

MARIAN: What even *is* a Zoom play? Is it a movie? No. Is it a TV show? Kinda, but no. Are there people watching? … Nobody knows!!! Wait, I can hear someone tapping a little happy face symbol now. What the fuck is this, Rose? It's madness! This isn't a play! It's a fucking nightmare.

ROSE: I swear to God if you start talking about Ibsen—

MARIAN: Ibsen could write women like nobody has ever written women. When I played Hedda Gabler in '76, I had men booing me from the back row and winking at me from the front. Lesbians too. Oh yes. Women's lib was huge then, so I took it as a compliment. At the stage door— this was in Westport, not Poughkeepsie— one of them threw her bra at me. Did I ever tell you this?

ROSE: Of course.

MARIAN: Then you know you're supposed to ask…

ROSE: "What did you do?"

MARIAN: I threw it back, in case later she needed to burn it! You're not laughing. I've done something wrong.

ROSE: You haven't done anything wrong.

MARIAN: Clearly I have. Look at your face.

ROSE: No, I've done something wrong.

MARIAN: Well don't be so hard on yourself. Everyone has to try their hand at writing a play sometime. I know I said I hadn't, but you know. Maybe I gave it a go once upon a time and hid it away in a drawer somewhere.

ROSE: My mistake was thinking that if I wrote a part for you, you'd— I don't know— we'd have fun or you'd— I don't know— appreciate my work. For once.

MARIAN: I appreciate your work. I'm here telling you how much potential you have!

ROSE: My potential is not me, Mom!

MARIAN: But it could be.

ROSE: You can't hear yourself?

MARIAN: Why are you casting me as the villain? I am your biggest fan, Rosie! *(pause, she takes another tack)* I know you wrote this part for me. She's a dynamo. She's got my voice. And for what it's worth, I think you nailed it.

ROSE: . . . Really?

MARIAN: Oh my god. Really? Yes really. It's so fun. First draft obviously. But you know that.

ROSE: Well, yeah.

MARIAN: But fun to speak. Very fun. You've a... a knack. For dialogue?

ROSE: You think so?

MARIAN: Absolutely. It comes from being raised in the theatre exposed to all the classics. You were always listening, always paying attention. Other kids weren't allowed in rehearsals. I said, Rosie's special. She's paying attention. And that does something to a child, right? To their development. Right?

ROSIE: Probably right.

MARIAN: Lucky girl.

ROSE: So, Mom? Do you . . .

MARIAN: Let's do it. Where should we go from?

ROSE: Uhm. Well, what if we—

MARIAN: A few beats back from where you got tongue tied.

ROSE: . . . Okay.

MARIAN: *(looks at watch)* Are we ready? From "what-do-you-want-Dena," Okay?

(Both take a moment to drop back into character: Marian as Cheryl the Senator and Rose as Dena the Staffer.)

CHERYL: What. Do you. Want, Dena?

DENA: I want to settle.

CHERYL: Okay. People in hell want an elevator pass. So?

DENA: I will settle.

CHERYL: For?

DENA: For an apology.

CHERYL: Uh. Huh. Huhuhu...haha! HAHAHAA! Yeah. I don't— I don't think that's going to happen, dear. No.

DENA: It's— It doesn't have to be public. I don't want it to be. Public I mean.

CHERYL: I don't care. ... What is it with your generation that the world owes you an apology. For what? For being hard? Life is hard. Bosses are hard. Especially if they give a damn, which is apparently my great mistake. I'm not going to apologize for caring about you, Dena. Sue me. ... Oh wait.

DENA: I'm sorry. You care about me? How is berating me into tears at Stanton's state dinner, caring? How is snide jokes about my wardrobe to your chief of staff? How is locking me in a car for five hours— that's called kidnapping— caring? How is disparaging and belittling my work at every possible turn… caring? You, myopic, twisted, narcissistic, bitter old …

CHERYL: Go ahead.

DENA: Battleaxe!

CHERYL: *(a beat)* Hm. That's not the 'B'-word I was expecting. *(sigh)* … Will you listen to me now?

DENA: You've done nothing but rant at me this whole—

CHERYL: Ah-ah-ahhh, just, just listen. Here's what is true. I do, in fact, care for you. And very much. *(She gathers herself.)* I often imagine— I sometimes entertain, a fear, that if I had had a daughter, this is how she would be treated. By me. How I've treated you; I would treat her.

DENA: You do have daughter.

CHERYL: But I mean one I like. A daughter I respected.

DENA: What are you saying?

CHERYL: I'm saying: you're right. I am hard. The world's hard? I'm hard. I am a battleaxe. I have to be. You girls today. When I came up, being respected meant being a man. Not being <u>like</u> a man. You had to

<u>be</u> a man. You had to eat men, consume them and wear their skins in the board room. You had to chop them off at the dick, and club them to death with their severed legs. I didn't have any teachers, any mentors. In 1965 my mother asked my father for her own credit card? He grounded her. I was hard on you? The reason was to toughen you up. I was hard on you because I was you. And I see what you could be. If you were tougher I mean. Oh Dena, what you could be.

DENA: What I <u>could</u> be.

CHERYL: You're so powerful. You're so smart. You don't even know.

DENA: I <u>do</u> know. I do know. You talk about respect, but then you come at me like you know who I am, as if <u>I</u> don't know who I am. I know who I am. And I don't have to wear anyone's else's skin to be me, because my skin suits me just fine. You— you respect what you think I <u>could</u> be. Listen to yourself. What I could be is not me. This is me. I am me. Seeing the person who is in front of you— that is respect. You say that you look at me, and you see yourself? Then I am very sorry. The way you treat me, you must absolutely despise yourself. You say you want to help, but what you do is you punish. You punish me because, I don't know, it's not as hard to be a woman as it used to be? Well, damn. With that kind of help, I'm lucky if I become anything at all. And if I do— when I do— it won't be because you. It will be in spite of you. So, Cheryl, if I really am this "daughter" you "like," then I don't think that's what you want to do. To torture me for being like you were. See, I think you're actually better than that. Oddly. And that is why we are talking at all. And that is why I am willing to settle… for an ap-ol-ogy. That is, if an apology is something of which you are at all familiar, or even capable.

(A long pause.)

CHERYL: I am. Familiar. … Capable? We'll see. But, you're right.

DENA: I know I am. . . . But, why would you say that?

CHERYL: What, that you're right?

DENA: Yes. That is very strange.

CHERYL: Because I listen, Dena. I listened, and I heard you. And I respect what you have said.

DENA: Well. Good.

CHERYL: And I'm not going to apologize.

DENA: Of course you're not.

CHERYL: Not right now. I want to think about it.

DENA: Really?

CHERYL: Yes. Really. Also, we have a fundraising deadline coming up, and your lawsuit is generating more donations than the last two SCOTUS rulings combined.

DENA: Oh, my god.

CHERYL: I know. You're like the liberal Alamo of the generational culture war.

DENA: The Alamo was propaganda.

CHERYL: How apropos. So we're gonna let this ride just another day. And also, I need to do some thinking. You are an impressive person, Dena Malloy. As you are. I was so focused on making you better than me; I didn't see that you already are. I hope they see you at that Disney ride they call a congressional campaign.

DENA: I think they do.

CHERYL: Alright. That's all the humanity that you're squeezing out of this bitter old battleaxe tonight. Are you satisfied?

DENA: No. I didn't get my apology.

CHERYL: Good girl.

DENA: Don't call me a girl.

CHERYL: *(nodding approval)* Good girl.

DENA: Goodnight, Senator.

(Dena motions as if to end the call.

They drop character, returning to ROSE & MARIAN.

During Rose's next speech, Marian looks off screen. We don't see that she's looking at her phone.)

ROSE: That's where Dan is gonna make our two screens go blank, so it's like the call ends? Then Brianne will come on and do a little Q&A thing. Oh my god you are so good in this. Thank you for doing it. Uhm, so I uh, I know you have to get going pretty soon here, but, if you have any thoughts, I mean especially on the ending, I'd—

MARIAN: *(Brings phone up to ear.)* Lois? Lois. I'm here but I don't want to rush. … Then you can wait, or I can meet you there. Okay. That's fine. *(Hangs up. To Rose?)* What, Rose?

ROSE: Huh? Oh. Thoughts?

MARIAN: Oh I'm late, Honey. This ran over. Send me all the details, okay?

(Marian nods, rises, and readies herself to go. She considers the call ended but doesn't bother closing the computer down. She goes on with her evening, collecting her things in the background.

Rose stares at the screen as she realizes this is all she has. After a long moment, after it's sunken in, she ENDS THE CALL.

END OF PLAY.)

About the Author

Jerrod Bogard's plays and musicals have been produced by professional theatres and community groups around the U.S. and internationally since 2006. His award-winning short films have been screened at film festivals nationally. He is a graduate of Florida School of the Arts and Brooklyn College and attended the BMI Lehman Engel Musical Theatre Workshop. He co-created and co-directed the playwright development program *'Wright Club* with The Amoralists in New York City. Bogard has created works commissioned by Theatre Breaking Through Barriers (TBTB) for invited performances at the United Nations in New York City and in Geneva, Switzerland. Bogard's work often focusses on socially conscious themes from a queer, working class perspective. As a director, playwright, and producer, he advocates for diverse casting in all his work including actors with disabilities and neurodivergence.

He is a father, husband, songwriter, puppeteer, meditator, social worker, Air Force brat, and a connoisseur of greasy spoon diners from coast to coast.

ENDNOTES

[1] Tomasello, Michael. "The Ultra-Social Animal." *European Journal of Social Psychology* 44, no. 3 (2014): 187–194. https://doi.org/10.1002/ejsp.2015.

[2] Frith, Uta, and Chris Frith. "The Social Brain: Allowing Humans to Boldly Go Where No Other Species Has Been." *Philosophical Transactions of the Royal Society of London. Series B, Biological Sciences* 365, no. 1537 (2010): 165–176. https://doi.org/10.1098/rstb.2009.0160.

[3] Broadway League. "Broadway Theatres To Suspend Performances Through April 12, 2020." Press release, March 12, 2020. https://www.broadwayleague.com/press/press-releases/broadway-theatres-to-suspend-performances-through-april-12-2020/.

[4] Influenza Encyclopedia. "New York, New York." https://www.influenzaarchive.org/cities/city-newyork.html.

[5] Americans for the Arts. "COVID-19's Pandemic's Impact on The Arts: Research Update May 12, 2022." https://www.americansforthearts.org/node/103614.

[6] University of Windsor. "This Weekend Is the Last Chance to Step Into the Stream with University Players." November 19, 2020. https://www.uwindsor.ca/dailynews/2020-11-18/weekend-last-chance-step-stream-university-players.

[7] Bogard, Jerrod. *Unmuted: four Zoom plays*. Denver: Moro Gem Publishers, 2026. xiv.

[8] Nelson, Richard. 2020. *What Do We Need to Talk About?* Broadway Play Publishing.

[9] Fuchs, Barbara. 2022. *Theater of Lockdown: Digital and Distanced Performance in a Time of Pandemic*. London, New York, Dublin: Methuen Drama. ISBN: 978-1-3502-3182-5.

[10] MacArthur, Michelle. "The Pedagogy of Grief: Lessons from Making Zoom Theatre During a Pandemic." *Canadian Theatre Review* 188, no. 1 (2021): 49–53. https://muse.jhu.edu/article/837167.

[11] Walsh, Fintan. "Grief Machines: Transhumanist Theatre, Digital Performance, Pandemic Time." *Theatre Journal* 73, no. 3 (2021): 391–407. https://doi.org/10.1353/tj.2021.0074.

[12] Collins-Hughes, Laura. "Digital Theater Isn't Theater. It's a Way to Mourn Its Absence." *New York Times*, July 8, 2020. https://www.nytimes.com/2020/07/08/theater/live-theater-absence.html.

[13] Gulkhara, Ahmadova, and Elza Farzaliyeva. 2025. "Theatre As a Reflection of Social Change: How Dramatic Arts Capture Cultural Shifts and Historical Transformations". *Acta Globalis Humanitatis Et Linguarum* 2 (1): 254-61. https://doi.org/10.69760/aghel.02500133.

[14] Winnicott, Donald W. 1960. "The Theory of the Parent-Infant Relationship." *International Journal of Psycho-Analysis* 41: 585-595.

[15] Compton, Timothy G. "Digitally-Delivered Mexican Theatre during the COVID-19 Pandemic of 2020." *Latin American Theatre Review* 54, no. 2 (2021): 199–215. https://doi.org/10.1353/ltr.2021.0009.

[16] Blair, Kelsey, et al. "From Site to Self: Immersion, Audience Research, and Polyvocality." *Journal of Dramatic Theory and Criticism* 36, no. 1 (2021): 75–93. https://doi.org/10.1353/dtc.2021.0034.

[17] Baird Television. "The First Television Production." https://www.bairdtelevision.com/1930.html.

[18] WGY / Albany Institute. "WGY Presented the First Ever Radio Drama, 'The Wolf,' in August 1922." https://www.albanyinstitute.org/online-exhibition/50-objects/section/wgy.

Thanks to: Mimi Bogard, Louis See, Christy Patti, Nick Basile, Nicholas Viselli, Ann Marie Morelli, Bennett Harrell, Ike, and Henry.